THE JUNIOR CHEF

In the same series

How To Boil An Egg

No Meat For Me, Please!

Microwave Recipes For One

All uniform with this book

THE JUNIOR CHEF

by

Jennie Daff

PAPERFRONTS
ELLIOT RIGHT WAY BOOKS
KINGSWOOD, SURREY, U.K.

Typeset in 10pt on 11pt Times by One & A Half Graphics, Redhill, Surrey.
Made and Printed in Great Britain by Richard Clay Ltd., Bungay, Suffolk.

CONTENTS

1

INTRODUCTION

FOR THE ADULT COOK

This book should be beneficial both to parents *and* children! It will help Mums or Dads who wish to introduce their children to cooking but often need ideas about what exactly to make, what methods and techniques to show and what will be interesting and fun to do, depending on the age and ability of the children. It will excite the children, who will begin to learn the art of creating delicious dishes from different kinds of ingredients. Often it will provide the answer when children have friends around in the holidays and say, "What can we do?"

Once children are familiar with the book and parents feel that they can handle equipment safely on their own, the keen ones will shortly take over the kitchen or be doing more and more without direct help! Sounder knowledge gained about weights and measures, health and well-being and food values and types, and a keener interest in different cooking methods and artistic creativeness are welcome extras.

I have tried to get away from the normal recipes associated with youngsters and attempted to introduce ingredients and ideas which will be completely new to most children, thus, I hope encouraging interest, curiosity and questions. Indeed I believe that the recipes are such that the book will find a permanent place on the kitchen bookshelf, whether the cook be seven or seventy and long after the initial learning days are over. However, not all the recipes are new. Some may be recognised as variations of perhaps temporarily forgotten old favourites from our Grandparents' or even Great Grandparents' days!

Another important aspect for most parents is cost. I have, I believe, been reasonably economical whilst not detracting from the character of the recipes, and in some cases have kept to smaller portions, as opposed to family sizes, to minimise expense. Other ways of keeping costs down are to buy the largest suitably sized packets and look for supermarket "own-brand" products. Don't buy fresh fruit and vegetables from the supermarket – go to your local market where they are usually cheaper and often fresher. Some other penny-pinching ways are to use block cooking chocolate (which is cheaper than any other form), coffee essence (which is cheaper than instant coffee) and rapeseed oil (which is also generally cheaper than other vegetable oils).

I have also aimed the book at school children of seven years and upwards, who are being supervised in groups by students, or volunteer parents, or teachers. I have made allowance for the shortage of equipment and space which may prevail, particularly in junior schools. Here too, the costs can be kept down if you bulk-buy the ingredients whenever possible and share the cost accordingly.

Whether the setting is in a school or in your own kitchen, I would advise working with groups of no more than six or eight children. Where a large quantity is made, such as biscuits like Christmas Stars (page 102), the task can be easily divided between two children once you reach a suitable stage – for example, before decorating.

Safety is an important aspect which must be dealt with right from the beginning. We must teach our children to "think safety". They should be supervised *at all times* and shown that special care is needed when using heat whatever its source – from the oven, a gas ring, electric element or microwave oven. The potential dangers of using sharp instruments must be stressed, i.e. knives, graters and tin openers. Just in case an accident does occur, have you got a first-aid kit in the kitchen and, perhaps more importantly, a fire blanket near the cooker – and do the children know where it is and how to use it? And don't forget also that "cleanliness is next to Godliness"!

As you can see (but may not have realised), teaching children to cook is a comprehensive subject, involving many hidden contributing factors. Nevertheless, these important points can quite easily be disguised as part of the fun and enjoyment of cooking, without teaching them solely and separately.

The book is divided according to the four seasons and I have tried wherever possible to associate recipes with events in the calendar, so that cooking can be linked with Easter, for example.

Each recipe has a simple indication of the cost, which I have divided into three different price levels denoted by £'s. One £ means economical, two ££ means reasonable and three £££ means a bit more expensive! This is all comparative within the book as my aim throughout has been economy.

Although most of the recipes are suitable for seven-year-olds there are a few which may prove a little difficult for these youngsters so this is indicated at the beginning of each recipe – use this as a guideline coupled with what you know of an individual child's capabilities.

I have given approximate preparation and cooking times at the start of each recipe, but obviously the actual preparation time it will take your child/children will ultimately depend upon the number of children in your group, their age and understanding. As many households now have freezers and microwave ovens, instructions are also given for these at the end of each individual recipe, where appropriate. There are also some notes and general guidelines for the use of these in relation to this book on pages 25 and 26.

Finally, I would like to thank the children especially, and the teachers, of Classes 5 and 7 of Stilton Primary School 1985/86, without whom this book would not have been born, as well as my long-suffering family for being "guinea-pigs" – still alive to tell the tale!

Happy cooking.

Jennie Daff

2

CONVERSION TABLES

As children are taught only metric measurements in school, the amounts given in the recipes in this book follow that system. I therefore set out below the relevant imperial equivalents which may be helpful to the supervisory generation. They are not precise conversions but have been rounded up or down.

Liquids		Solids	
fl. oz.	*ml.*	*oz.*	*grams*
2	55	½	10
3	75	1	25
5 (¼ pt)	150	1½	40
10 (½ pt)	300	2	50
15 (¾ pt)	450	2½	60
20 (1 pt)	600	4	100
1¾ pints	1 litre	6	150
		8	225
		12	350
		16 (1 lb)	450

Measurements		**Measurements**	
inch	*mm/cm*	*inch*	*mm/cm*
⅛	3mm	7	18cm
¼	5mm	8	20cm
½	1cm	9	23cm
¾	2cm	10	25½cm
1	2½cm	11	28cm
2	5cm	12	30cm
3	7½cm		
4	10cm		
5	13cm		
6	15cm		

Oven Temperatures

Gas mark	Electric Fahrenheit	Celsius
¼	225°F	110°C
½	250	130
1	275	140
2	300	150
3	325	170
4	350	180
5	375	190
6	400	200
7	425	220
8	450	230
9	475	240

Level spoonfuls are used in the recipes, except where specified otherwise.

3

COOKING EQUIPMENT YOU WILL NEED

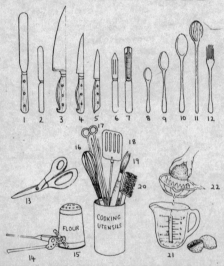

Fig. 1. Cooking equipment and utensils you will need

1. Palette knife
2. Table knife
3. Chopping knife
4. Sharp knife
5. Vegetable knife
6. Vegetable peeler
7. Apple corer
8. Teaspoon
9. Dessertspoon
10. Tablespoon
11. Wooden spoon
12. Fork
13. Kitchen scissors
14. Tin opener
15. Flour dredger
16. Whisk
17. Skewers
18. Egg slice
19. Pastry brush
20. Vegetable brush
21. Measuring jug
22. Lemon squeezer

Fig. 2. Cooking equipment you will need
1. Chopping board
2. Colander
3. Frying pan
4. Saucepans
5. Kitchen scales
6. Sieve
7. Grater
8. Bowls
9. Basins
10. Egg whisk

Fig. 3. Cooking equipment you will need

1. Sponge tin
2. Flan tin
3. Cake tin
4. Baking tray
5. Bun tin
6. Swiss roll tin
7. Pastry cutters
8. Rolling pin and pastry board
9. Ruler
10. Oven gloves
11. Cake cooling rack
12. Paper cake/sweet cases

4

HEALTH AND FOOD VALUES

To help us grow, to be fit and healthy, we need a varied diet containing:

Carbohydrates – a main source of energy, found in: bread, pasta, cereals, root vegetables (e.g. potatoes, carrots), fruit (both fresh and dried) and sugar.

Fats – another main source of energy, found in: butter, oils, milk products, eggs, meat and nuts.

Proteins – the body builders, also giving some energy, found in: meat, fish, milk, cheese, eggs, bread, cereals, pasta and vegetables.

Minerals and Vitamins – generally keep our bodies healthy and prevent diseases (e.g. those affecting the eyes, bones and teeth, skin, digestive or nervous systems) and are found in: vegetables, cereals, fish, meat and milk products.

Fibre – is important for the digestive system, found in: bread, cereals, nuts, fruit and vegetables.

A good rule to remember is to vary your diet as much as possible. The old saying "a little of what you fancy does you good" is the one to be noted, remembering the moderation!

5

SAFETY FIRST

A kitchen can be a dangerous place if you do not use your common sense. Always "think safety" and concentrate on what you are doing. However careful you are, these safety rules should always be remembered.

1. NEVER touch electrical equipment with wet hands, i.e. cookers, plugs, electric kettles, etc.

2. KEEP all towels and tea towels away from gas rings and heating elements.

3. ALWAYS light a gas oven or gas ring quickly before the gas builds up and make sure all the flames are lit properly.

4. MAKE SURE that the oven or cooking rings (gas or electric) are fully turned off as soon as you have finished with them.

5. HEAT IS DANGEROUS – always check that you have a clear heat-resistant surface (i.e. a surface that won't be damaged by heat) to put hot things on *before* you open the oven door.

6. ALWAYS use proper oven gloves to take things in and out of the oven, and make sure you don't drop anything on your feet (or knees if you are kneeling down to open the oven door). OVEN DOORS often get very hot so be careful when near them.

7. REMEMBER tins and dishes hold their heat for some

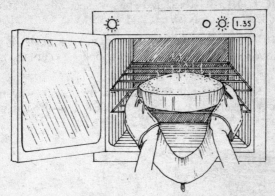

Fig. 4. Taking things out of the oven

time after being removed from the oven and food that has been microwaved stays very hot much longer – it goes on cooking.

8. **USE** proper oven gloves when lifting any lid from saucepans or casserole dishes – beware of steam – it scalds!

9. **ALWAYS** make sure that saucepan and frying pan handles are turned towards the back of the cooker, so that they cannot be knocked off by accident or pulled down by any baby brother or sister.

10. **ALWAYS** hold the handle of a saucepan/frying pan with your free hand when stirring the contents.

Fig. 5. Stirring a saucepan and holding it with your free hand

11. HOT OIL BURNS, and spits – especially if water is added to it, so NEVER add water to it.

12. NEVER go away and leave anything cooking on the stove – not even to answer the telephone. Turn the heat off first.

13. TAKE CARE with sharp knives; always cut away from your fingers or body and NEVER fool around with them.

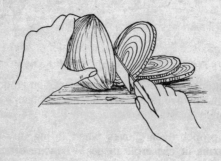

Fig. 6.   Cutting away from your fingers

14. GRATERS are sharp – mind your fingers!

15. NEVER mess around with plastic bags or leave them where younger children (who don't understand the danger of suffocation) might play with them.

6

COOKING WORDS

Bake Blind – to bake without the filling.

Beat – to mix briskly, usually with a wooden spoon, turning the mixture over and over.

Beaten egg – to break the shell open, put the egg into a small basin or cup and to break up and mix the yolk and white together with a fork so that it can be mixed into other ingredients more evenly.

Bind – to mix ingredients to hold them together firmly.

Blend – to mix ingredients evenly to remove all lumps.

Boil – to cook in liquid at a minimum temperature of 100°C (212°F) when the surface will be bubbling hard all the time.

Consistency – the texture (thickness) of a mixture.

Core – to take out the central part of certain fruits (such as apples) which hold the seeds.

Cream – to beat ingredients, usually fat and sugar, to the consistency of thick cream.

Defrost – to thaw.

Dice – to cut into even cube-shaped pieces.

Essence – a concentrate of flavouring.

Flake – to break up gently into small thin pieces with a fork.

Flouring a pastry board – to sprinkle or sieve flour lightly over the board to prevent the food sticking when it is rolled out.

Fold in – to add ingredients to a light, whipped or beaten mixture carefully without knocking the air out, so that it keeps its lightness.

Glaze – to coat with egg, sugar or jam to give a shine and prevent the top drying out.

Grease tins – to use a brush dipped in oil and paint all over the inside surfaces of tins to prevent the mixture sticking.

Hull – to pull out the stalks and green bits from strawberries, raspberries, blackberries.

Knead – to combine, with your hands, a mixture which is too stiff to stir.

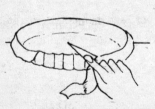

Line (a flan tin or bun tins) – to place rolled-out pastry so that it covers the inside (bottom and sides) of the tin in one piece, and trimming it to fit.

Marinade – to soak food in a liquid to add flavour and make it tender.

Melt (chocolate, margarine) – to put into a basin in small pieces and place over a saucepan of hot but *not* boiling water on a gentle heat until smooth and runny.

Open Freeze – to place item(s) on a baking sheet without touching each other, and freezing in the fast freeze compartment/shelf, before packing.

Pinch (of salt) – to pick up a measure of salt between finger and thumb.

Purée – to put fruit (usually cooked) or vegetables through a sieve to make a smooth, thick mixture.

Root vegetables – vegetables whose edible parts grow in the soil, i.e. potatoes, turnips, swedes, parnsips, carrots.

Rub-in – to mix fat into flour gently using fingertips, until it looks and feels like fine breadcrumbs.

Season – to add salt and pepper, and sometimes herbs, spices, etc. to give flavour to a dish.

Separate eggs – to crack the shell open and to part the yolk from the white.

Shred – to cut or tear into long narrow strips.

Sieve or Sift – to put dry ingredients through a sieve to remove any lumps, and to add air.

Simmer – to cook, on a gentle heat, not quite boiling. There should be an occasional bubble.

Stock – a liquid in which meat, fish, bones or vegetables have been simmered for a long time to bring out their flavours. Widely available in the concentrated form of "cubes". To make stock by using a stock cube: crumble the cube into a measuring jug, add the required amount of boiling water, and stir with a spoon so that the cube dissolves.

Thaw – to melt – become unfrozen.

Zest – the coloured part of the rind of citrus fruits (oranges, lemons, limes) which holds the flavour.

7

ALWAYS REMEMBER TOO ...

... wash your hands before handling food.

... tie back long hair.

... make sure work surfaces and floor are clean before you start cooking – wipe away any spills immediately they occur.

... wear an apron to protect your clothes – all the famous cooks do!

... put the oven on first. Some electric ovens take about 15 minutes to reach temperature – gas is quicker. Microwave ovens do not need pre-heating.

... read right through a recipe before you start, to check that you have all the ingredients and equipment together first, and to get an idea of the order of method.

...always wash fruit and vegetables well in cold water before using them, to rinse away any sprays that have been used on them.

... wash up as you go along – it's not so bad that way.

... enjoy your cooking.

8

FREEZING

The easiest way to preserve food is by freezing. With most of the recipes in this book you can put any left-overs in the freezer for emergencies. Bake two – eat one and freeze one.

Some basic rules to remember when freezing food are:

1. Only freeze food in fresh, perfect condition.

2. Make sure that cooked foods are cold before freezing.

3. Seal food in airtight materials, e.g. aluminium foil, polythene bags, freezer wrap, plastic boxes, waxed containers.

4. Secure the package and label it clearly with the details of contents and date of freezing.

5. Keep a freezer diary, listing contents and dates of freezing, so that you know what you have in your freezer and when it should be used. Freezing times are stated on each recipe where suitable.

The best way to THAW food from the freezer is in the refrigerator overnight, or longer if need be. A quicker, quite acceptable way is to thaw at room temperature away from direct heat. You can also thaw in a microwave oven speedily, but you should follow the oven manufacturer's instructions in their handbook.

9

MICROWAVING

As microwave ovens are becoming more and more popular I have given the appropriate details at the end of the conventional cooking methods wherever a recipe is suitable for microwaving. These ovens perform extra tasks such as thawing and melting, as well as reheating, in a matter of seconds and minutes as opposed to the minutes and hours of conventional cooking. As a general guide, microwaving takes a quarter to a third of the conventional cooking time, depending on how much food is to be cooked, its starting temperature and density. It is important with this method of cooking *not* to give an extra minute or two to cook "just to make sure it's done", but to allow for "standing time". This means that food cooked by microwaves continues to cook for 5-10 minutes after the oven is turned off, so it is best to test the food after the standing time, and if it is not quite cooked to microwave it for a few seconds more.

Test if food is cooked
Some foods look different when cooked by microwaves from conventionally cooked foods. Cakes and sponges may look wet on the surface but will dry during the standing time. Test by inserting a wooden cocktail stick into the centre; it should come out clean and the sides of the sponge will come away from the cooking container when it is cooked.

Custards, quiches and egg-based flans will look soft in the centre. Test by inserting a knife about halfway between the centre and the outside edge; it should come out clean when the dish is cooked.

Pastries will not brown but should look dry when cooked.

Vegetables should feel tender when tested with a fork.

Jacket potatoes should remain firm at the end of cooking time. Wrap in foil and leave to stand for about 5 minutes.

Suitable containers

Special microwave cookware is not necessary as many items in your kitchen may be used safely, such as Pyrex and plain glass, china, pottery, earthenware, even basketware, paper plates and some plastics.

A simple test to check the suitability of a container if you are uncertain is to put the dish in the microwave together with a glass of water and microwave on HIGH for about 1½ minutes. If the water feels hot and the dish cool, it is suitable. If the dish feels warm and the water cool, it is *not* suitable.

Containers made of aluminium, copper, stainless steel or tin, or with a metal trim (including gold decoration) and tin foil should *not* be used as these may damage the oven.

The best results are gained by using a round container with straight sides. Oval dishes allow food at the narrow ends to cook more quickly and containers with sharp square corners are not so good as ones with slightly rounded corners, as the food overcooks in these areas thus giving uneven cooking. Sponges cooked by microwave ovens need deeper containers than in conventional cooking as they rise quicker and higher – always only half fill them.

The finished look

Food cooked in a microwave also differs from conventional cooking because it does not brown. To get around this, you may either use a special microwave browning dish, or allow for it in the recipes by using some suitable colouring method, e.g. for cakes and puddings add spices, dark brown sugar, black syrup, cocoa, gravy browning, or sprinkle with a mixture of sugar and spice, toasted coconut, chopped nuts, vermicelli, etc., or cover with a coloured frosting or icing. For savoury dishes, brush or coat with tomato, brown or

Worcester sauces. Alternatively, pop under a pre-heated grill for 2-3 minutes after cooking.

Foods not suitable for microwaving

Eggs cannot be boiled, nor whole cooked eggs reheated.

Deep fat frying of chips or really crisp foods like roast potatoes.

Yorkshire puddings and other batter mixes.

Biscuits will not crisp.

Pastry with filling enclosed, e.g. sausage rolls, pies, etc.

Rich fruit cakes made by the creaming method.

Meringues.

Cooking times

The recipes in this book have been tested with a 500 watt output microwave with a built-in turntable. Actual cooking times vary according to the starting temperature, quantity, thickness and density of the food, and the types of container, its size and shape. The times stated in these recipes are to be used as a guide – consult your manufacturer's handbook for further information. If in doubt always under cook – extra time can be added – but not taken away!

For a 600 watt oven *decrease* the cooking time by 20 seconds for each minute in the recipes.

For a 700 watt oven *decrease* the cooking time by 40 seconds for each minute in the recipes.

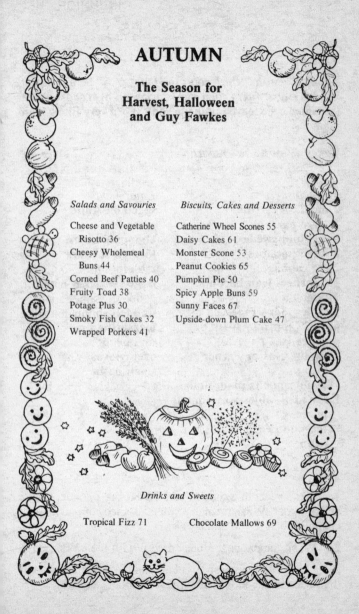

AUTUMN

The Season for
Harvest, Halloween
and Guy Fawkes

Salads and Savouries

Cheese and Vegetable
   Risotto 36
Cheesy Wholemeal
   Buns 44
Corned Beef Patties 40
Fruity Toad 38
Potage Plus 30
Smoky Fish Cakes 32
Wrapped Porkers 41

Biscuits, Cakes and Desserts

Catherine Wheel Scones 55
Daisy Cakes 61
Monster Scone 53
Peanut Cookies 65
Pumpkin Pie 50
Spicy Apple Buns 59
Sunny Faces 67
Upside-down Plum Cake 47

Drinks and Sweets

Tropical Fizz 71   Chocolate Mallows 69

POTAGE PLUS

Cost: ££   *Age: 7+*

"Potage" means "thick soup" and the "plus" here is bacon,
but this is also a very good way of using left-over cooked meat
(in which case leave out the bacon). It is a very filling main
meal.

Takes 40 mins. to prepare   *Serves 4-6*
        30 mins. to cook

You will need: *Equipment:*
2 medium carrots   **vegetable knife**
1 large parsnip   **colander**
1 medium swede   **chopping board**
2 large potatoes   **kitchen scissors**
250g cabbage   **tablespoon**
4-6 rashers lean bacon   **large saucepan with**
1 large onion   **lid**
2 tablespoons rapeseed oil   **wooden spoon**
600ml (approx.) stock or   **measuring jug**
    water (see page 23)   **tin opener**
142g tin peas or French   **oven gloves**
    beans   **small basin**
1-2 tablespoons plain flour
1 rounded tablespoon tomato
    purée
½ teaspoon each of salt and
    pepper

Method
1.   Use a vegetable knife to peel the carrots, parsnip, swede
and potatoes. Wash them in a colander, then chop them on a
chopping board into small dice.

2.   Wash the cabbage, then shred it with the knife.

3.   Using kitchen scissors, cut any rind from the bacon, and
then cut the bacon into small pieces about 1cm wide.

4. Peel and chop the onion.

5. Heat the oil in a saucepan over a medium heat for a minute or two and then fry the bacon and onion until they begin to brown, stirring with a wooden spoon as you go along to prevent sticking.

6. Add the diced vegetables and then enough stock or water so that it almost covers them. Stir well and bring the whole lot to the boil. Cover with the lid, reduce the heat to low and simmer for about 10 minutes until the vegetables are almost tender. (Test for softness by sticking the point of a sharp knife in some of the pieces; if the knife comes out easily then it is ready.)

7. Use an oven glove to remove the lid *(remember that steam scalds – take care)*. Add the cabbage and tinned vegetables. Replace the lid and cook for a further 4-5 minutes.

8. Meanwhile, blend 1 heaped tablespoonful of flour with 3 tablespoonfuls of cold water in a small basin until smooth.

9. Keep the potage simmering while you add your blended flour and stir continuously with the wooden spoon until it thickens. The potage should be thick; if it doesn't thicken fairly quickly, make up a little more blended flour and add to it.

10. Finally add the tomato purée, salt and pepper, and stir well.

Serve immediately with fresh bread rolls.

To freeze
Cool, then pour into a plastic container. Cover with a lid, label, and freeze for up to 3 months.

To serve from frozen
Leave in the refrigerator overnight, pour into a saucepan and heat gently until simmering, stirring occasionally. Simmer for 4-5 minutes until heated through. Alternatively, reheat gently directly from frozen.

SMOKY FISH CAKES

Cost: £££   *Age: 11+*

These tasty fish cakes are made with smoked fish instead of
the usual white fish.

Takes 35 mins. to prepare   *Serves 4*
         25 mins. to cook

You will need: *Equipment:*
350g potatoes   potato peeler
225g smoked cod OR haddock   vegetable knife
1 tablespoon fresh chopped   chopping board
    parsley OR 2 teaspoons   medium saucepan with
    dried parsley   lid
Salt and pepper   large saucepan with
1 size 4 egg, beaten   lid
                                    oven gloves
Coating: colander
½ size 4 egg, beaten   3 large plates
50g breadcrumbs   potato masher or fork
                                    2 small dishes
2-3 tablespoons oil   frying pan
                                    egg slice
                                    kitchen paper

Method
1.   Peel the potatoes and then wash them and cut them into
small even-sized pieces.

2.   Place them in a medium-sized saucepan and pour in
enough cold water just to cover them. Put on the lid, place
over a high heat and bring to the boil, then turn the heat to low
and simmer for about 10 minutes until cooked. They should
feel soft when tested with a sharp knife.

3. Meanwhile, put the fish into a large saucepan, cover with cold water and the lid, and place on a high heat to bring to the boil. Turn the heat to low and simmer for 10-15 minutes until cooked. It should look a creamy colour and break up easily.

4. Use the oven gloves to remove the lid *(take care – remember steam scalds)*. Drain the fish into a colander and then place it on a large plate and leave to cool.

5. Drain the potatoes in the colander and then return them to their saucepan and mash with a potato masher or fork.

6. When the fish is cold, flake it off into very small pieces, carefully removing any skin and bones.

7. Add the fish to the mashed potato with the parsley, a pinch of salt and 2 or 3 pinches of pepper and bind together with the whole egg.

8. Put the egg for coating into a small dish and the breadcrumbs into a separate dish.

9. To make the cakes, take a rounded tablespoonful of the fish and potato mixture and form into a flattened round with your hands. Place on a plate. Repeat with the rest of the mixture, making 8 fish cakes.

10. To coat the fish cakes, first dip one into the egg, turning it over with a fork. Drain off the excess and then dip it in the breadcrumbs, turning to coat all over. Place on a plate and repeat with the rest of the fish cakes (see fig. 19 overleaf).

(If microwaving, go to Stage 6 of the Microwave Method.)

Fig. 19. Dipping the fish cake

11. Put the oil in a frying pan over a medium heat for about 2 minutes to get hot and then fry the fish cakes for about 5-10 minutes until crisp and brown on both sides, turning them over with an egg slice half-way through the cooking time.

12. Drain on absorbent kitchen paper and serve hot.

To freeze
After Stage 10, before cooking: open freeze on a baking tray until solid and then pack into a plastic box or bag. Seal, label and freeze for up to 3 months.

To serve from frozen
Fry in hot oil over a medium heat for 8-10 minutes, turning occasionally. No need to thaw first.

To microwave   *Takes 35 mins. to prepare*
                                   17 mins. to cook
1. Put the fish in a suitable shallow dish and pour 50ml of water over.

2. Cover the dish and microwave on HIGH for 4-5 minutes or until the fish looks creamy and flakes when tested with a fork. Leave to cool.

3. Peel and wash the potatoes, cut them into small pieces and place them in a microwave-proof dish with 4 tablespoons of water.

4. Cover and cook on HIGH for 7-9 minutes until tender. Drain, put into a large bowl and mash with a potato masher or fork.

5. Follow Stages 6-10 of the Conventional Cooking Method.

6. To cook, place 4 on a plate at a time, put a dot of margarine on the top of each one and microwave on HIGH for 1½ minutes, turn them over and repeat. Serve hot.

To microwave from frozen
Place 4 on a plate at a time and microwave on HIGH for 3¼ minutes, stand for 3 minutes and then microwave for a further 1¼ minutes.

CHEESE AND VEGETABLE RISOTTO

Cost: ££   *Age:* 7+

A tasty vegetarian dish, this is good as a snack or supper-time meal. The cheese should be just melting but still chunky.

Takes 20 mins. to prepare   *Serves 2*
*   25 mins. to cook*

You will need: *Equipment:*

1-2 tablespoons rapeseed oil   1 tablespoon
**   OR margarine   saucepan (1.5 litre)**
1 medium onion, chopped   with lid
100g long grain brown rice   chopping board
1 medium carrot, chopped   vegetable knife
300ml stock OR water, hot   scales
**   (see page 23)   wooden spoon**
75g sweetcorn, tinned   measuring jug
75g peas, tinned   oven gloves
100g Cheddar cheese   tin opener
salt and pepper
2 tablespoons fresh parsley,
**   chopped**

Method

1.   Put the oil into a saucepan over a medium heat for 2-3 minutes. Add the onion and fry until soft but not brown.

2.   Add the rice and carrot and stir with a wooden spoon for a minute. Then add the hot stock or water, stir again, cover with the lid and simmer for 10-15 minutes or until all the stock has been soaked up.

3.   Use the oven gloves to remove the lid *(take care – remember steam scalds).* Add the sweetcorn and peas, stir and cook for a further 1-2 minutes. Meanwhile, cut the cheese into 1cm cubes.

4. Stir in a pinch of salt and a little more of black pepper. Add the cheese. Turn off the heat after 1-2 minutes, before the cheese melts completely.

5. Sprinkle with fresh parsley.

Serve hot or cold, with a green salad and fresh crusty bread.

To freeze
At Stage 3, before cutting the cheese: cool, pour into a plastic container, seal, label and freeze for up to 3 months.

To serve from frozen
Put into a saucepan with 1 tablespoon of water, cover with a lid and heat gently, stirring occasionally, until it simmers. After 2-3 minutes add the seasoning and cheese as at Stage 4.

To microwave   *Takes 20 mins. to prepare*
                                               13 mins. to cook
                                            5-10 mins. to stand

1. Put the oil into a casserole dish and microwave for 1½ minutes on HIGH. Add the onion and cook for 2½ minutes on HIGH.

2. Stir in the rice and carrot and boiling stock or water. Cover and microwave for 8 minutes on HIGH, or until all the stock has been soaked up.

3. Remove the cover and stir in the sweetcorn and peas, salt and pepper.

4. Cut the cheese into 1 cm cubes and add to the casserole. Microwave, uncovered, on HIGH for 1 minute and then cover and leave to stand for 5-10 minutes.

Serve hot or cold, with a green salad and fresh crusty bread.

To microwave from frozen
Put into a casserole dish and microwave on DEFROST for 6 minutes, and then cook on HIGH for 12 minutes, stirring twice.

FRUITY TOAD

Cost: ££   *Age:* 7+

This variation of an old favourite – Toad-in-the-hole – has added apple and onion.

Takes 20 mins. to prepare   *Serves 4*
     50 mins. to cook

You will need: *Equipment:*

100g plain white flour   scales
1 egg, size 4   mixing bowl
280ml milk   sieve
2 tablespoons rapeseed oil   wooden spoon
5 pork sausages   measuring jug
1 small onion   tablespoon
1 dessert (eating) apple   deep tin or ovenproof
                                        dish (22-24cm long)
                                    chopping board
                                    vegetable knife
                                    oven gloves

Method
1. Set the oven to 425°F (220°C, gas Mark 7).
2. Make the batter – sieve the flour into a mixing bowl,

Fig. 20. Making the batter

make a well in the centre and put the egg in with a little milk. Beat with a wooden spoon, gradually working the flour down from the sides of the bowl and, at the same time, adding the rest of the milk little by little, beating until smooth. Leave on one side.

3. Put the oil into the tin/dish and heat in the oven for about 5 minutes until very hot – it should be just beginning to smoke.

4. Meanwhile, using a vegetable knife and chopping board, cut the sausages into bite-size pieces. Peel, wash and chop the onion finely.

5. Remove the dish from the oven *very carefully*. Put the sausage pieces and onion in the hot oil (REMEMBER HOT FAT SPITS AND BURNS – TAKE CARE). Return the dish to the oven for 5 minutes until the sausages begin to brown.

6. Peel, core, and thinly slice the apple and sprinkle it amongst the sausage pieces. Carefully pour in the batter.

7. Bake for about 20-25 minutes until well risen and golden. Then reduce the heat to 375°F (190°C, gas mark 5) for 10-15 minutes to cook through the centre.

Serve immediately with green vegetables.

CORNED BEEF PATTIES

Cost: £   *Age: 7+*

A scrumptious puff pastry case around a corned beef filling
with just a hint of horseradish and apple. These are good for
lunch boxes and parties.

Takes 1 hour to thaw the pastry   *Makes 9*
*   20 mins. to prepare*
*   15 mins. to cook*

You will need: *Equipment:*

225g frozen puff pastry,   scales
     thawed   pastry board
100g corned beef   rolling pin
3 teaspoons horseradish   flour dredger
     cream   7½cm pastry cutter
50g cooking apple   bun tin (for 9 buns)
pepper   tin opener
milk to glaze   basin
                                      fork
                                      teaspoon
                                      vegetable knife
                                      chopping board
                                      pastry brush
                                      oven gloves
                                      cooling rack

Method
1.   Leave the pastry to thaw at room temperature for about
1 hour before you want to use it.

2.   Set the oven to 450°F (230°C, gas mark 8).

3.   When the pastry is completely thawed, sprinkle flour
from a flour dredger onto a pastry board (to prevent the
pastry sticking to it), and roll out the pastry thinly. Cut

9 rounds with the pastry cutter and line the bun tin with them. Keep the rest of the pastry for later.

4. Carefully open the can of corned beef. Put the corned beef into a basin and mash with a fork and then mix in the horseradish.

5. Using a vegetable knife and chopping board, peel, core and finely chop the apple and add it to the meat with a pinch or two of pepper. Mix well.

6. Fill the bun tins with the mixture, firming it down slightly with the back of a spoon.

7. Re-roll the remaining pastry and cut an equal number of lids and cover the buns with them. Brush over with a little milk to glaze.

8. Bake in the centre of the oven for 10-15 minutes until golden brown.

Serve hot or cold.

To store
In the refrigerator for 2-3 days.

To freeze
Cool, freeze in the tin, remove when solid and pack in a polythene bag or plastic box. Seal, label and freeze for up to 4 months.

To serve from frozen
Return it to the bun tin and reheat for about 20-25 minutes at 400°F (200°C, gas mark 6).

WRAPPED PORKERS

Cost: ££   *Age: 7+*

Sausage rolls with a tasty pastry, using wholemeal flour, cheese and herbs.

Takes 30 mins. to prepare   *Makes 8*
15 mins. to cook

You will need: *Equipment:*
50g wholemeal flour   **scales**
50g plain white flour   **tablespoon**
1 teaspoon baking powder   **mixing bowl**
1 teaspoon dry mustard   **sieve**
50g hard margarine   **teaspoon**
50g Cheddar or Leicester   **table knife**
** cheese**   **grater**
½ teaspoon basil, dry   **small basin**
1 egg, size 4   **fork**
1-2 teaspoons cold water   **pastry board**
8 skinless pork sausages   **flour dredger**
                                    rolling pin
                                    palette knife
                                    pastry brush
                                    baking tray
                                    oven gloves
                                    cooling tray

Method

1.   Set the oven to 400°F (200°C, gas mark 6).

2.   Sift the flours, baking powder and mustard into a mixing bowl, add the margarine (cut into small pieces) and rub in until it resembles fine breadcrumbs.

3.   Grate the cheese finely *(mind your fingers – graters are sharp!)* and add it with the basil to the ingredients in the mixing bowl, then mix it in.

4.   Break the egg into a small basin and beat it lightly with a fork. Reserve about 1 tablespoonful of the egg for glazing and add the rest to the dry ingredients and mix to a soft, but not sticky, dough (1-2 teaspoons of cold water may be needed to achieve this).

5.   Sprinkle flour from a flour dredger onto a pastry board. Turn the dough onto the floured board and knead gently until smooth.

6. Roll it out into a neat oblong, ½cm thick and about 8cm wide.

7. Cut off pieces at 5cm intervals with the palette knife. (These pieces should now be 8cm x 5cm). Place a sausage across each one.

8. Starting from a short side, roll up each piece of pastry over a sausage to overlap, leaving the sausages sticking out of

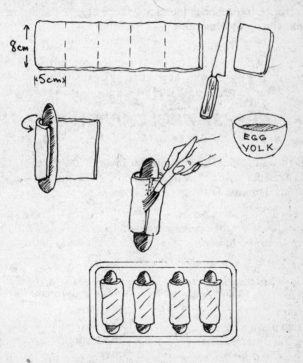

Fig. 21. Rolling the pastry round
the sausages

both ends. Brush the overlapped ends of pastry with a little of the reserved egg to seal the join.

9. Place on a baking tray with the joins underneath, put 3 or 4 knife marks across the tops of the rolls for decoration and brush with the rest of the egg to glaze.

10. Bake for 15 minutes in the centre of the oven until golden brown.

Serve warm or cold.

To freeze
Cool, open freeze, pack into a polythene bag, seal, label and freeze for up to 4 months.

To serve from frozen
Take out of the bags and leave at room temperature for about 2 hours. The pastry may need crisping again in the oven for about 10 minutes at 350°F (180°C, gas mark 4).

CHEESY WHOLEMEAL BUNS

Cost: £   *Age: 7+*

This is a quick and easy recipe for bread without yeast. It's also a chance to use your imagination to make animal shapes such as Tommy Tortoise or Cuthbert Cat!

Takes 20 mins. to prepare   *Makes 4 large buns*
(plus 10 mins. for the tortoise/cat)
and 25 mins. to cook

You will need:
225g wholemeal flour
1 teaspoon bicarbonate of soda
½ teaspoon salt
50g hard margarine
100g Cheddar cheese
150ml milk

Equipment:
scales
mixing bowl
tablespoon
teaspoon
table knife
grater
measuring jug
pastry board
flour dredger
baking tray
pastry brush
oven gloves

Method

1.   Preheat the oven to 400°F (200°C, gas mark 6).

2.   Put the flour, bicarbonate of soda and salt into a bowl, add the margarine (cut into small pieces) and rub in until the mixture resembles fine breadcrumbs.

3.   Finely grate the cheese *(mind your fingers – graters are sharp!),* add to the flour and mix to a dough with most of the milk, making sure that it doesn't get too sticky. (Add a little more milk if necessary).

4.   Cut into 4 equal pieces. Sprinkle flour from a flour dredger on a pastry board, and gently knead each piece of dough on the board into a large round, flattening slightly to about 2cm thick.

5.   Place on a baking tray and cook for 25 minutes.

Serve warm or cool on a wire tray.

To make 4 tortoises

At Stage 4, divide the dough into 4 equal pieces, then divide each of these into 6 pieces as follows: a big piece for the body (about half of it), then a piece for the head (about one third of the body size), and 4 legs slightly smaller than the head. Assemble them on a baking tray, brushing the areas which join together with a little milk to help them to stick together. Make a shell pattern with a knife. Bake for about 20 minutes.

To make 4 cats

At Stage 4, divide the dough into 4 equal pieces, then divide

Fig. 22. The tortoise and the cat

each of these into a small ball for the head, a large ball (about three times bigger than the head for the body), a long sausage-shaped tail and then 2 little pieces for the ears. Brush the joining areas with a little milk to make them stick together. Put 3 currants in the head to represent the eyes and nose and put 6 short lengths of spaghetti for whiskers. Bake for about 20 minutes.

To freeze
Cool, pack in polythene bags, seal, label and freeze for up to 6 months.

To serve from frozen
Place on a baking tray while still frozen and bake in a preheated oven for 10-15 minutes at 400°F (200°C, gas mark 6).

UPSIDE-DOWN PLUM CAKE

Cost: £   *Age: 7+*

Serve this hot as a pudding, or cold as a cake.

Takes 25 mins. to prepare   *Serves 6*
      1 hour to cook

You will need: *Equipment:*

50g soft margarine   deep round ovenproof
50g soft brown sugar   dish (18cm diameter)
½ teaspoon mixed spice   scales
225g plums (Victoria)   table knife
100g soft margarine   oven gloves
100g white sugar   2 tablespoons
2 eggs, size 4   teaspoon
75g wholemeal flour   vegetable knife
75g plain white flour   mixing bowl
1 level teaspoon baking   wooden spoon
   powder   sieve
3 tablespoons milk   serving plate

Method
1.   Preheat the oven to 325°F (170°C, gas mark 3-4).

2.   Put 50g of the margarine in the dish and put in the oven for about 5 minutes until melted. Remove from the oven. Stir in the 50g of brown sugar and the spice.

3.   Wash the plums, cut them in half lengthways and remove the stones.

4.   Put the plums in the base of the dish, with the cut sides downwards. Leave on one side.

5. Make the sponge. Put the margarine and sugar into a mixing bowl and beat together with a wooden spoon until soft and creamy.

6. Add the eggs, one at a time, and beat well after each one.

7. Sieve the flours and baking powder into the mixture and fold it in. Finally mix in the milk.

8. Spoon the mixture on top of the fruit and make it level.

(If microwaving, go to Stage 3 of the Microwave Method.)

9. Bake in the centre of the oven for about 1 hour until golden on the top and springy to touch.

10. To turn out – place a serving plate upside-down on top of the dish and then, carefully holding the dish and plate together with the oven gloves, turn it upside-down so that the pudding comes to rest on the plate.

Serve hot or cold with yoghurt or cream.

To freeze
Wrap in foil first and then a plastic bag. Seal, label and freeze for up to 3 months.

To serve from frozen
To serve cold, unwrap and leave at room temperature for about 4 hours. To serve warm, reheat directly from frozen at 325°F (170°C, gas mark 3) for about 30-45 minutes.

To microwave   *Takes 20 mins. to prepare*
                                            13 mins. to cook
                                            5 mins. to stand

1. Put 50g of margarine in a deep microwave-proof dish and microwave on HIGH for 1 minute so that it melts. Stir in the 50g of brown sugar, and the spice.

2. Follow Steps 3-8 of the Conventional Cooking Method.

3. Microwave on HIGH for 12 minutes or until the cake feels dry to touch. Leave to stand for 5 minutes. Then to turn out, put the serving plate upside-down on top of the dish and carefully, holding the dish and plate together, turn them upside-down so that the pudding comes to rest on the plate.

Serve hot or cold with yoghurt or cream.

PUMPKIN PIE

Cost: ££   *Age: 9+*

Try this instead of an apple pie for a change. It has a delicious
light creamy filling.

Takes 45 mins. to prepare   *Serves 6*
45 mins. to cook

You will need: *Equipment:*

1 kg pumpkin   vegetable knife
50g wholemeal flour   chopping board
150g plain white flour   saucepan
125g hard margarine   2 sieves
1 tablespoon white sugar   2 small bowls
1 egg yolk, size 4   2 mixing bowls
1 tablespoon cold water   tablespoon
1 teaspoon ground nutmeg   scales
½ teaspoon mixed spice   table knife
75g mixed peel   pastry board
3 eggs, size 4   flour dredger
50g-100g white sugar   rolling pin
                                  deep round pie
                                     dish (22cm)
                                  fork
                                  teaspoon
                                  baking tray
                                  oven gloves

Method
1.   Preheat the oven to 375°F (190°C, gas mark 5).

2.   Peel the pumpkin with a vegetable knife, remove the
seeds and chop the flesh into chunks. Put into a saucepan and

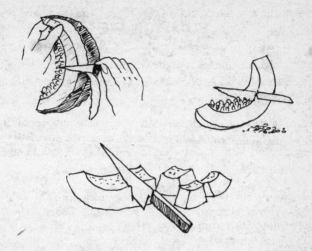

Fig. 23. Peeling, de-seeding and chopping the pumpkin

almost cover with cold water. Place on a high heat and bring
to the boil, then reduce the heat to simmer for about 10-15
minutes, until cooked.

3.   Pour into a sieve so that it strains into a small bowl.
Leave to cool.

4.   Make the pastry – sieve the flours into a mixing bowl,
add the margarine (cut into small pieces), and rub in until
crumbly.

5.   Add 1 tablespoon of sugar and stir, then bind together
with the egg yolk and water to form a firm dough.

6.   Sprinkle flour from a flour dredger onto a pastry board.
Turn the dough onto the board and roll it out thinly. Line the
pie dish with it. Leave on one side.

7.   Put the drained pumpkin into the second mixing bowl

and mash with a fork. Stir in the spices. Add the mixed peel
and stir in.

8. Break the eggs into the remaining small bowl, beat well
with a fork and then add to the pumpkin. Stir in about 50g of
the sugar and taste, adding more if required.

9. Pour into the pastry case.

10. Roll out the remaining pastry and place it on top of the
pie, trimming the edges to fit. Gently press the edges all the
way around, with your finger, to seal. Make 3 small cuts in
the lid for the steam to escape.

11. Place the dish on a baking tray and bake for about
45 minutes.

Serve hot with cream or yoghurt.

To freeze
Open freeze and then carefully remove from the dish. Wrap
in foil, then a plastic bag. Seal, label and freeze for up to
4 months.

To serve from frozen
Unwrap and return to the original dish. Put into a preheated
oven at 425°F (220°C, gas mark 7) for 20 minutes, then
reduce the heat to 375°F (190°C, gas mark 5) for a further 20
minutes. Cover with foil if it starts to brown too much.

MONSTER SCONE

Cost: £   *Age: 7+*

This is a large fruit scone. Use your imagination to create a monster with the dates.

Takes 20 mins. to prepare   *Serves 4*
*   15 mins. to cook*

You will need:	*Equipment:*
50g plain white flour	**scales**
50g wholemeal flour	**tablespoon**
2 teaspoons baking powder	**mixing bowl**
25g hard margarine	**sieve**
¼ teaspoon nutmeg, freshly grated	**teaspoon**
	grater
25g soft dark brown sugar	**table knife**
25g dried apricots, chopped	**pastry board**
4-5 tablespoons milk	**flour dredger**
dates for face	**egg slice**
milk for glazing	**baking tray**
	vegetable knife
	pastry brush

Method

1.   Preheat the oven to 425°F (220°C, gas mark 7).

2.   Sieve the flours and baking powder into a mixing bowl, add the margarine (cut into small pieces) and rub in until the mixture is crumbly.

3.   Mix in the nutmeg, sugar and apricots. Add most of the milk, stirring it with a knife – be careful not to use too much milk, the dough should not be sticky, just soft.

4.   Sprinkle flour from a flour dredger onto a pastry board. Turn the dough onto the board and knead it gently until smooth. Shape into a roughly round shape with your hands, about 1cm thick.

Fig. 24. Suggested shapes

5. Lift onto a baking tray with an egg slice and make a monster face, with the dates representing eyes, nose and fangs! Use a vegetable knife to cut the shapes.

(If microwaving, go to Stage 2 of the Microwave Method.)

6. Brush the scone with milk and then bake for 15 minutes or until it is well risen and golden. Serve warm with a little butter. It's best eaten the same day.

To freeze
Cool, open freeze and pack in foil or a plastic bag. Seal, label and freeze for up to 3 months.

To serve from frozen
Remove the wrapping and place on a baking tray. Cover with foil and reheat at 400°F (200°C, gas mark 6) for about 15 minutes.

To microwave   *Takes 20 mins. to prepare*
                                        7 mins. to cook
1. Follow Stages 2-5 of the Conventional Cooking Method, but use a plate instead of a baking tray.

2. Microwave on HIGH for 4-5 minutes and then brush with a little milk and brown under a hot grill for 1-2 minutes.

Serve warm with a little butter. Best eaten same day.

CATHERINE WHEEL SCONES

Cost: £   *Age: 7+*

These are delicious straight from the oven, spread with a little butter.

Takes 30 mins. to prepare   *Makes 12*
*   20 mins. to cook*

You will need: *Equipment:*

oil for greasing   sandwich tin (20cm)
100g wholemeal flour   pastry brush
100g plain white flour   scales
2 level teaspoons baking   2 tablespoons
   powder   mixing bowls, large
50g hard margarine   and small
150ml milk   sieve
25g margarine, to be melted   teaspoon
50g soft brown sugar   table knife
1 level teaspoon cinnamon   measuring jug
50g currants   pastry board
                              flour dredger
                              rolling pin
                              ruler
                              small saucepan
                              palette knife
                              oven gloves

Method
1.   Preheat the oven to 425°F (220°C, gas mark 7). Grease the sandwich tin.

2.   Sieve the flours into a large mixing bowl with the baking powder.

3.   Add the margarine (cut into small pieces), and rub in until it resembles fine breadcrumbs.

4.   Add the milk and mix to a soft, not too sticky, dough, with a table knife.

5.   Sprinkle flour from a flour dredger onto a pastry board. Turn the dough onto the board and knead it gently and then roll it into an oblong about 30 x 20cm.

(If microwaving, go to Stage 2 of the Microwave Method.)

6.   Put the 25g margarine into a small saucepan and heat gently over a low heat until melted, then brush it all over the rolled-out dough.

7.   In a small bowl, mix together the sugar, spice and currants, then sprinkle this over the dough, leaving 1 cm free on both long sides.

8.   Beginning with a long side, roll up like a Swiss roll, using the palette knife to help you.

Roll up like
a Swiss roll

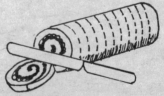

Cut into slices

Put into a tin

9. Cut the roll into 12 equal slices and place them in the tin, horizontally (cut sides upwards).

10. Bake near the top of the oven for 15-20 minutes. Pull apart while still warm and serve with butter.

Best eaten the same day.

To freeze
Cool, pack in a plastic bag (keeping them in the tin), seal, label and freeze for up to 3 months.

To serve from frozen
Remove from the bag and place the tin in a preheated oven 425°F (220°C, gas mark 7) for 15 minutes. (Cover with foil if they begin to brown too much.)

To microwave   *Takes 30 mins. to prepare*
                                           5 mins. to cook
                                        10 mins. to stand

Add 15g more hard margarine making 65g in total.

Use only ¾ teaspoon of cinnamon instead of 1 level teaspoon.

1. Follow Stages 2-5 of the Conventional Cooking Method.

2. To melt the margarine, put it in a small basin and microwave on HIGH for a few seconds. Stir. Repeat the process until it is melted, and then brush all over the dough.

3. In a small basin, mix together the sugar, ¾ teaspoon of spice and the currants and then sprinkle this over the dough leaving 1cm free on both long sides.

4. Beginning with a long side, roll the dough up like a Swiss roll, using the palette knife to help you.

5. Cut the roll into 12 equal slices and place in a microwave-proof dish.

6. Microwave on HIGH for 5 minutes, then leave to stand for 10 minutes.

Pull apart while still warm and serve with butter.

SPICY APPLE BUNS

Cost: £   *Age:* 7+

Cox's Orange Pippin apples give a distinctive flavour to these moist and spicy buns. They are ideal for picnics and lunch boxes.

Takes 25 mins. to prepare   *Makes 8*
       15 mins. to cook

You will need: *Equipment:*
50g soft margarine   **bun tin (for 8 buns)**
50g white sugar   **8 paper cake cases**
1 egg, size 4   **scales**
50g wholemeal flour   **mixing bowl**
50g plain white flour   **2 tablespoons**
1 teaspoon baking powder   **table knife**
½ teaspoon ground   **wooden spoon**
**   cinnamon**   **teaspoon**
½ teaspoon ground   **sieve**
**   nutmeg**   **vegetable knife**
1-2 tablespoons milk   **chopping board**
75g chopped apple   **small bowl**
2 teaspoons white sugar   **oven gloves**
1 teaspoon mixed spice   **cooling rack**

Method
1.   Preheat the oven to 425°F (220°C, gas mark 7). Put 8 paper cake cases in a bun tin.

2.   Put the margarine and sugar into a mixing bowl and cream together with a wooden spoon until light and fluffy.

3. Add the egg and beat in well. Sieve the flours, baking powder, cinnamon and nutmeg, then fold them into the mixture, together with the milk.

4. If using an eating apple, wash, core and chop it finely and then mix it into the bun mixture. If using a cooking apple, first peel it, then core and finely chop it and add it to the mixture.

5. Place 1 level tablespoonful of the mixture in each cake case.

6. In a small bowl, mix together 2 teaspoons of sugar with 1 teaspoon of mixed spice and then sprinkle this over the top of each bun.

7. Bake in the centre of the oven for 15 minutes until golden and well risen. Cool on a wire tray.

To store
In an airtight tin for 4-5 days.

To freeze
Cool, place in plastic bags, seal, label and freeze for up to 6 months.

To serve from frozen
Remove from bag and leave at room temperature for 1-2 hours.

DAISY CAKES

Cost: £   *Age: 10+*

Individual chocolate and orange-flavoured cakes. The decoration is a bit fiddly, but effective; it takes a bit longer than other recipes so you may want to do only half the quantity or share this with a friend.

Takes 1 hour to prepare   *Makes 12 cakes*
15 mins. to cook

You will need: *Equipment:*

75g soft margarine   **12-hole bun tray**
75g white sugar   **12 paper cake cases**
1 egg, size 4   **mixing bowl**
50g wholemeal flour   **scales**
50g white flour, plain   **table knife**
1 level teaspoon baking   **tablespoon**
   powder   **wooden spoon**
2 tablespoons orange squash   **sieve**
   concentrate   **teaspoon**
40g plain chocolate,   **grater**
   grated   **oven gloves**
Buttercream and decoration: **cooling rack**
40g soft margarine   **2 small bowls**
75g icing sugar   **scissors**
1 teaspoon cocoa   **jug**
orange flavouring and
   colouring
marshmallows and "Smarties"

Method
1.   Set the oven to 350°F (180°C, gas mark 4). Put the

paper cake cases in the bun tray.

2. Put the margarine and sugar into a mixing bowl and cream together with a wooden spoon until soft and light.

3. Add the egg and beat it in. Sieve the flours and baking powder and fold them into the mixture. Fold in the orange squash and chocolate.

4. Divide the mixture between the cake cases and bake for about 12-15 minutes until golden.

5. Cool completely on a wire rack before decorating.

6. Make the buttercream – put the remaining margarine and the icing sugar into a bowl and beat together until smooth and creamy.

7. Put half of the buttercream into a separate bowl and flavour it with the cocoa, adding 1 teaspoon of water. Beat until smooth.

8. Flavour the other half with 3-4 drops of orange essence and add 3-4 drops of orange colouring.

9. When the cakes are cold, spread the chocolate buttercream over the tops of 6 of the cakes and the orange-flavoured buttercream over the tops of the remaining 6 cakes.

10. To make the "petals", cut the marshmallows into 3 or 4 pieces horizontally, then cut each of these in half. (It is much easier if you keep wetting the scissors in a jug of water to prevent them sticking.)

11. Place one sweet "Smartie" in the centre of each cake and then five marshmallow petals around this. Repeat with all the cakes.

To store
In an airtight tin for 5-7 days.

To freeze
Open freeze, then pack into plastic bags or boxes. Seal, label and freeze for up to 3 months.

To serve from frozen
Unwrap and leave at room temperature for 1-2 hours.

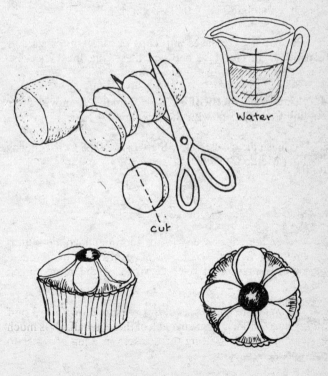

Fig. 26. Making the petals

To microwave   *Takes 1 hour to prepare*
                                  7 mins. to cook

You need a tablespoonful of milk for this.

1.   Put the margarine and sugar into a mixing bowl and beat until soft and light.

2.   Add the egg and beat it in. Sieve the flours and baking powder and fold them into the mixture. Fold in the orange squash, chocolate and 1 tablespoon of milk.

3.   Put paper cake cases into cups or ramekin dishes and then divide the mixture between these, making 12 cakes. Place these on a plate – 6 at a time.

4.   Microwave on HIGH for 3-3½ minutes. Remove onto a cooling tray. Repeat with the remaining 6 cakes.

5.   To finish the cakes, follow Steps 6-11 of the Conventional Cooking Method.

PEANUT COOKIES

Cost: ££   *Age:* 7+

These are a great favourite with children of all ages!

Takes 25 mins. to prepare   *Makes about 28*
    10 mins. to cook

You will need:	*Equipment:*
75g soft margarine	mixing bowl
75g demerara sugar	tablespoon
75g white sugar	table knife
1 egg, size 4	scales
75g plain white flour	wooden spoon
1 level teaspoon bicarbonate	sieve
of soda	teaspoon
75g porridge oats	plastic bag
3 level tablespoons peanut	tie-tag
butter	rolling pin
50g honey roast peanuts	baking trays
	oven gloves
	palette knife
	wire tray

Method

1.   Preheat the oven to 350°F (180°C, gas mark 4).

2.   Put the margarine and both sugars into a mixing bowl and beat together with a wooden spoon. Add the egg and beat until smooth.

3.   Sieve the flour and bicarbonate of soda into the mixing bowl and mix together.

4.   Add the oats and mix again.

5.   Add the peanut butter and mix well in.

6.   Put the nuts into a plastic bag, secure the opening with a tie-tag, and then crush by gently tapping them with a rolling pin. Undo the bag, add the nuts to the mixture and mix well in as shown overleaf.

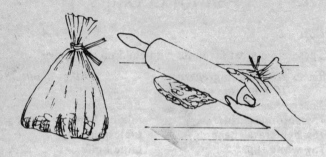

Fig. 27. Crushing the nuts

7.   Place teaspoonfuls of the mixture on baking trays and flatten slightly with the back of the spoon, leaving space between them to spread slightly during cooking.

8.   Bake for about 10 minutes until golden. Leave on the trays for 5 minutes and then transfer, using a palette knife, to a wire cooling tray.

To store
In an airtight tin for up to about 2 weeks – if they're not eaten first.

SUNNY FACES

Cost: £   *Age:* 7+

These shortbread biscuits, sandwiched with lemon curd, are
fun to make into happy faces.

Takes 35 mins. to prepare   *Makes about 14*
       20 mins. to cook

You will need: *Equipment:*

150g plain white flour   **scales**
50g white sugar   **tablespoon**
100g hard margarine   **sieve**
1 teaspoon grated lemon zest   **mixing bowl**
2 level tablespoons lemon   **table knife**
   curd   **grater**
                                  pastry board
                                  flour dredger
                                  rolling pin
                                  plain biscuit cutter
                                     (4½cm)
                                  palette knife
                                  baking tray
                                  teaspoon
                                  pointed knife
                                  oven gloves
                                  cooling rack

Method

1.   Set the oven to 350°F (180°C, gas mark 4).

2.   Sift the flour into a mixing bowl and stir in the sugar.

3.   Add the margarine, cut into small pieces, and rub in with your fingertips until the mixture is crumbly.

4.   Carefully grate the zest from the lemon *(mind your fingers!),* add to the mixture and mix in.

5.   Knead the mixture together with your hand to form a fairly firm dough, leaving the bowl clean.

6.   Sprinkle flour from a flour dredger onto a pastry board. Turn out the dough onto the board and roll it out quite thinly (about 3mm).

7.   Using the biscuit cutter, cut out as many rounds as you can, and then gather up the left-overs and repeat the process.

8.   Using a palette knife, place half of the circles on a baking tray and spread about half a teaspoon of lemon curd over, almost to the edges.

9.   Make the remaining half of the circles into faces: using the tip of a sharp knife, cut out small circles for eyes and happy mouth shapes underneath.

Fig. 28. Making the faces

10. Place these on top of the lemon curd-covered halves and gently press around the edges to seal them.

11. Bake for 20 minutes until golden.

12. Leave on the baking tray for 5 minutes and then lift onto a wire cooling rack with a palette knife.

To store
These will keep for up to about 2 weeks in an airtight container.

CHOCOLATE MALLOWS

Cost: £   *Age: 7+*

These are scrumptious! Very quick and easy to make too.

Takes 25 mins. to prepare   *Makes 20-22*

You will need:	Equipment:
50g cooking chocolate (plain or milk)	**scales**
	small saucepan
25g (approx.) coconut	**small bowl**
25g (approx.) chopped nuts	**3 small dishes**
10g (approx.) cereals (crispies or cornflakes)	**tablespoon**
	fork
1 packet marshmallows	**greaseproof paper**
	table knife

Method
1.   Break the chocolate into small pieces and put them into a small bowl fitted over a pan of hot water on a low heat so that they melt (see page 21), stirring with a table knife until smooth.

2. Pour some coconut and chopped nuts into separate dishes.

3. Put some cereals into another separate dish and gently crush them with the back of a spoon.

4. Push a fork into the base of a marshmallow (not quite all the way through) and dip it into the melted chocolate, turning to coat the top and sides.

Fig. 29 Stages 4 and 5

5. Roll it immediately in *one* of the coatings (coconut, nuts or cereals), and then place on the greaseproof paper to set.

6. Vary the coatings; do some of each.

To store
If these do not get eaten immediately they will keep in an airtight container as long as you like!

To make a present
These make a delightful gift for your favourite aunt or granny! A pretty cup and saucer make good packaging – just

fill the cup with the sweets, cover with cling film and perhaps add a pretty ribbon bow.

Fig. 30. Making a present

To microwave – takes 25 mins. to prepare.
The chocolate may be melted in a bowl for about 2 minutes on MEDIUM. Stir with a knife and then follow the instructions above.

TROPICAL FIZZ

Cost: £   *Age: 7+*

Delicious!

Takes 5 mins. plus chilling time   *Serves 4-5*

You will need:	Equipment:
250ml mixed fruit juice	**measuring jug**
1 litre bottle lemonade	**mixing bowl**
orange, lemon and lime	**tablespoon**
** slices**	**vegetable knife**

Method
1.   Chill the fruit juice before using it.

2.   Put the fruit juice into a large bowl and stir in the lemonade.

3.   Carefully cut a few thin slices horizontally across an orange, a lemon and a lime, and float these on top of the juice. Serve immediately.

Other variations
Try using a diluted chilled jelly such as strawberry, blackcurrant or black cherry, mix with lemonade and top with a spoonful of ice-cream so that it melts into the drink.

WINTER

The Season for Christmas, Warm Snacks and Valentines

Salads and Savouries

Baked Potatoes 75

Bean Cheese Crumble 77

Chicken Pasta 79

Spaghetti Bake 81

Winter Salad 74

Biscuits, Cakes and Desserts

Alphabet Cookies 100

Apple Charlotte Layer 83

Apple Oat Crumble 89

Christmas Buns 93

Christmas Igloo Cake 96

Christmas Stars 102

Fruit Fool 90

Mince Pies 92

Sunshine Scone Pizza 86

Sweets

Chocolate Coconut Ice 106   Fruit and Nut Clusters 108

Fondants 104

WINTER SALAD

Cost: £   *Age:* 7+

This is a cheap and cheerful salad for winter when lettuce and tomatoes are usually expensive.

Takes 35 mins. to prepare   *Serves 6-8*

You will need:	*Equipment:*
225g hard white cabbage	**scales**
1 medium onion	**colander**
2 carrots	**chopping board**
1 tablespoon lemon juice	**vegetable knife**
1 dessert (eating) apple	**mixing bowl**
3 sticks celery	**grater**
50g raisins	**small dish**
25g nuts, chopped	**tablespoon**
283g low calorie salad dressing	**large serving dish**

Method

1.   Wash the cabbage in a colander and cut (shred) it with a vegetable knife into long thin strips on a chopping board. Place them in a large mixing bowl.

2.   Peel, wash and finely chop the onion. Add to the cabbage.

3.   Wash, scrape and grate the carrots into the cabbage. *(Mind your fingers – graters are sharp!)*

4.   Put the lemon juice in a small dish, then wash, core and chop the apple and toss it immediately in the lemon juice to prevent it browning.

5.   Wash and finely chop the celery and add to the cabbage.

6.   Add the raisins and nuts and mix it all together.

7.   Add just enough salad dressing to coat the vegetables, mixing it thoroughly. (It will need almost all of the bottle.) Pour into an attractive serving dish.

Fig. 31. Tossing the apple in the lemon juice

Serve with a baked potato (see next recipe) and cold cut meats or a pork pie.

To store
In the refrigerator covered with cling film, for 3-4 days.

BAKED POTATOES

Cost: £   *Age: 7+*

This is a very versatile recipe with endless variations – try some of your own favourites.

Takes 10 mins. to prepare   *Serves 2*
1 hour 10 mins. to cook

You will need:	*Equipment:*
2 medium potatoes	**vegetable brush**
50g onion	**fork**
50g mushrooms	**baking tray**
25g margarine	**oven gloves**
2 tablespoons peas, cooked	**scales**
	vegetable knife
	chopping board
	frying pan
	egg slice
	mixing bowl
	tablespoon

Method

1.   Preheat the oven to 375°F (190°C, gas mark 5).

2.   Scrub the potatoes with a vegetable brush, dry them and then prick them all over with a fork.

3.   Place them on a baking tray and bake for about 1 hour. Test with a skewer, or the point of a knife, pushed into the middle of the potato – if it feels soft, then it is cooked.

4.   Peel and finely chop the onion with a vegetable knife. Wipe over the mushrooms with a clean, damp cloth and slice them.

5.   Put the margarine in a frying pan over a medium heat until melted and then add the onion and mushrooms and fry until the onions begin to turn golden, stirring occasionally with an egg slice. Remove from the heat.

6.   Cut the potatoes in half lengthways and scoop out the potato from the skins into a bowl. Pour the contents of the frying pan into the bowl, add the peas and mix well together.

7.   Return the mixture to the potato skins, replace on the baking tray and return to the oven until heated through – about 10 minutes.

Serve immediately.

To microwave   *Takes 10 mins. to prepare*
                                  19 mins. to cook

1.   Scrub and dry the potatoes and then prick them all over with a fork.

2.   Place them on absorbent kitchen paper on a plate and microwave on HIGH for 5 minutes, turn them over and cook for a further 5 minutes. Leave to stand for 5 minutes.

3.   Meanwhile, put the margarine in a microwave-proof

bowl and microwave for 1 minute on MEDIUM so that it melts. Peel and finely chop the onion, wipe over and slice the mushrooms and add to the margarine. Cover and cook on HIGH for 5½ minutes until soft.

4. Cut the potatoes in half lengthways and scoop out the potato from the skins and add to the onion and mushrooms.

5. Add the peas and mix well together.

6. Return the mixture to the skins, place on a serving plate and microwave for 3 minutes on MEDIUM to reheat.

Serve immediately.

BEAN CHEESE CRUMBLE

Cost: £   *Age: 7+*

Another different way of using a tin of beans.

Takes 20 mins. to prepare   *Serves 4*
*   40 mins. to cook*

You will need: *Equipment:*
3-4 rashers lean bacon   **kitchen scissors**
447g tin baked beans   **sharp knife**
2 teaspoons dried chives   **chopping board**
25g plain white flour   **tin opener**
75g porridge oats   **1½ litre ovenproof**
¼ teaspoon black pepper   **   dish**
50g Cheddar or Cheshire   **teaspoon**
**   cheese**   **tablespoon**
40g margarine   **scales**
                                    mixing bowl
                                    sieve
                                    grater
                                    small saucepan
                                    oven gloves

Method
1. Preheat the oven to 400°F (200°C, gas mark 6). Preheat the grill to a medium heat.

2.   Cut the rind off the bacon with kitchen scissors. Grill the bacon on both sides until turning golden. Cut it with a sharp knife on the chopping board into bite-size pieces.

3.   Carefully open the tin of beans *(keep your fingers away from the sharp edges)* and put them into an ovenproof dish. Mix in the bacon pieces and chives.

4.   Make the crumble – sieve the flour into a mixing bowl, add the oats and black pepper and mix together with a tablespoon. Finely grate the cheese into the bowl and mix in. *(Make sure you don't cut your fingers on the grater).*

(If microwaving, go to Stage 4 of the Microwave Method.)

5.   Put the margarine in a small saucepan over a low heat so that it melts. Stir it into the dry ingredients and mix well.

6.   Sprinkle the crumble mixture over the beans to cover them and bake in the oven for 30 minutes until golden brown. Serve hot with a green salad.

To microwave   *Takes 20 mins. to prepare*
                                    20 mins. to cook

1.   Cut the rind off the bacon with kitchen scissors. Put the bacon in a single layer on a plate or microwaving rack, cover with a piece of absorbent kitchen roll and cook on HIGH for 4½-5 minutes. Cut into bite-size pieces.

2.   Carefully open the tin of beans and pour into a 1½ litre microwave-proof dish. Mix in the bacon pieces and chives.

3.   Follow Stage 4 of the Conventional Cooking Method.

4.   Put the margarine into a small bowl and microwave on HIGH for a few seconds to melt. Stir into the dry ingredients and mix well. Sprinkle the crumble mixture over the beans to cover.

5.   Microwave on HIGH for 12½ minutes, and then brown under a preheated grill for 2-3 minutes. Serve hot.

CHICKEN PASTA

Cost: £   *Age: 7+*

This .delicious supper dish uses up left-over chicken or turkey. Bacon or cooked ham could be used instead.

Takes 20 mins. to prepare   *Serves 4*
   20 mins. to cook

You will need: *Equipment:*
1 medium onion   chopping board
275-350g cooked chicken OR   vegetable knife
   turkey   scales
225g pasta spirals (preferably   measuring jug
   wholewheat)   large saucepan
1 tablespoon vegetable oil   wooden spoon
25g margarine   colander
salt and black pepper   tablespoon
3 tablespoons grated   frying pan
   Parmesan cheese

Method
1.   Peel and finely chop the onion, using a vegetable knife and chopping board, then chop the chicken or turkey meat into bite-size pieces.

2.   Put about 2½ litres of cold water into the saucepan and bring to the boil over a high heat.

3.   Gradually add the pasta (remember STEAM SCALDS). Stir with a wooden spoon, bring back to the boil and then turn the heat to low to simmer for 10 minutes, stirring 2 or 3 times. Drain in a colander.

(If microwaving, go to Stage 1 of the Microwave Method.)

4.   Meanwhile, put the oil into a frying pan over a medium heat for about 2 minutes until hot and then add the onion and fry until beginning to turn golden, stirring occasionally.

5. Add the margarine to melt it and then add the cooked meat and heat for 2-3 minutes, stirring.

6. Turn the heat down to low, and add the drained pasta and cook for about 4-5 minutes, until warmed through, stirring frequently to prevent any sticking to the pan.

7. Season with a pinch of salt and 2 or 3 pinches of pepper (more if you like). Finally add the Parmesan cheese, mix well and serve immediately.

Serve with fresh crusty bread and more Parmesan for sprinkling over.

To microwave   *Takes 20 mins. to prepare*
                                  16 mins. to cook

As the pasta takes as long to cook by microwaves as by the conventional method, follow Stages 2 and 3 above and then continue as follows:

1. Peel and finely chop the onion, using a vegetable knife and chopping board. Roughly chop the chicken or turkey meat into bite-size pieces.

2. Put the oil into a large bowl with the onion and cook on HIGH for 5 minutes, stirring once.

3. Add the margarine and cooked chicken or turkey, stir, cover and cook on HIGH for 6 minutes.

4. Add the drained pasta, stir, cover again and heat for about 5 minutes on HIGH until it starts to steam.

5. Season with a pinch of salt and 2 or 3 pinches of pepper (more if you like). Finally add the Parmesan. Stir well and serve immediately.

SPAGHETTI BAKE

Cost: £   *Age: 7+*

This makes a delicious supper or tea-time dish. For a main meal, add sausages or beefburgers, fresh salad and crusty bread.

Takes 25 mins. to prepare   *Serves 2-3*
         22 mins. to cook

You will need: *Equipment:*

100g spaghetti   **saucepan (4 litre)**
225g onions   **scales**
25g margarine   **colander**
1 tablespoon vegetable oil   **chopping board**
230g tin tomatoes   **vegetable knife**
175g Cheddar or Cheshire   **tablespoon**
  cheese   **frying pan**
                                    tin opener
                                    wooden spoon
                                    grater
                                    1½ litre ovenproof
                                        dish
                                    oven gloves

Method
1.   Preheat the oven to 425°F (220°C, gas mark 7).

2.   Just over half fill the saucepan with cold water, put it on a high heat and bring to the boil. Meanwhile, break the spaghetti into shorter lengths and then very carefully put it into the boiling water (remember STEAM SCALDS). Bring back to the boil and then reduce the heat to simmer for about 10 minutes until tender. Drain in a colander.

3. Peel and slice the onions into rings, using a vegetable knife and chopping board.

4. Put the margarine and oil in a frying pan over a medium heat for 1-2 minutes until hot and then add the onion and fry until soft.

5. Carefully open the tin of tomatoes *(remember sharp edges cut!)*, add to the onions and stir with a wooden spoon.

6. Carefully grate the cheese *(mind your fingers!)*.

7. Assemble the ingredients in layers in an ovenproof dish – first put half of the spaghetti, followed by half of the cheese

Cheese
Spaghetti
Tomato/Onion
Cheese
Spaghetti

Fig. 32. The various layers

and then all of the onion and tomato mixture. Then put the rest of the spaghetti and top with the rest of the cheese.

8. Bake in the oven for 10 minutes.

Serve hot.

To microwave   *Takes 25 mins. to prepare*
                                               27 mins to cook

Note: It is at least as quick to cook the pasta by the conventional method as by microwaving.

1. Put the spaghetti (broken into shorter lengths) into a large bowl and pour over 500ml of boiling water, stir and then cover and microwave on HIGH for 16 minutes, stirring once or twice. Leave to stand.

2. Put the margarine and oil into a dish and microwave on HIGH for 1 minute.

3. Peel and chop the onion into rings, using a vegetable knife and chopping board, and add to the oil, cover and microwave for 6 minutes on HIGH.

4. Carefully open the tin of tomatoes and add to the onion and mix together.

5. Carefully grate the cheese *(mind your fingers!)*.

6. Drain the spaghetti in a colander.

7. Assemble the ingredients in layers in a microwave-proof 1½ litre dish – first half of the spaghetti, then half of the cheese followed by all of the onion and tomato mixture. Then the remaining half of spaghetti and finish with the rest of the cheese.

8. Microwave on HIGH for 3½ minutes.

Serve hot.

APPLE CHARLOTTE LAYER

Cost: £   *Age: 7+*

Charlotte is not only a girl's name but also means a dessert made with fruit and layers (or casing) of bread or sponge. This Charlotte is a little spicy.

Takes 40 mins. to prepare   *Serves 4*
25 mins. to cook

You will need: *Equipment:*
675g cooking apples   **scales**
3 tablespoons brown sugar   **sharp knife**
3 tablespoons water   **chopping board**
1 teaspoon lemon juice   **saucepan with lid**
4 thick slices brown bread   **tablespoon**
75g margarine   **grater**
50g brown sugar   **frying pan**
3 teaspoons ground cinnamon   **2 wooden spoons**
                                    teaspoon
                                    deep glass serving dish

Method

1. Peel, core and chop the apples, using a sharp knife and a chopping board. Put them into a saucepan, add 3 tablespoons of brown sugar, the water and lemon juice. Cover with the lid and cook on a gentle heat for about 20 minutes or until tender, stirring occasionally with a wooden spoon.

2. Cut the crusts off the bread and grate the slices into crumbs. *(Make sure you don't cut your fingers on the grater.)*

Fig. 33. Grating the bread

3. Put the margarine into a frying pan over a gentle heat so that it melts and then add the breadcrumbs and fry until crisp, turning occasionally with a wooden spoon.

4. Add the remaining brown sugar and the spice, remove from the heat and mix well.

5. Put a layer of the apple into the glass serving dish, then a layer of the crumbs, keeping it level. Repeat until it is all used – ending with a layer of the crumbs.

Fig. 34. Layers

6. Leave to cool and then chill in the refrigerator.

Serve with natural yoghurt.

To freeze
Freeze the apples in a plastic box and freeze the breadcrumbs separately in a plastic bag. Seal, label and freeze for up to 1 month.

To serve from frozen
Remove the lid from the packaging, undo the plastic bag and leave at room temperature for about 2 hours and then assemble as Stage 5 above.

To microwave   *Takes 40 mins. to prepare*
                                  15 mins. to cook

1. Peel, core and chop the apples (using a sharp knife and a chopping board), and put them into a deep microwave-proof dish with the brown sugar (3 tablespoonfuls), water and lemon juice. Microwave on HIGH for 8-10 minutes, stirring occasionally.

2. Continue as from Stage 2 in the Coventional Cooking Method.

SUNSHINE SCONE PIZZA

Cost: £   *Age: 7+*

This sweet pizza has a quick scone base and makes an
economical dessert.

Takes 25 mins. to prepare   *Serves 5-6*
20 mins. to cook

You will need: *Equipment:*
50g wholemeal flour   **scales**
50g plain white flour   **mixing bowl**
1½ teaspoons baking powder   **sieve**
25g hard margarine   **tablespoon**
50g white sugar   **teaspoon**
4 tablespoons milk   **table knife**
200g tin peaches, drained   **pastry board**
312g tin mandarins, drained   **flour dredger**
                                           rolling pin
                                           ruler
                                           egg slice
                                           baking tray
                                           tin opener
                                           oven gloves

Method

1.   Preheat the oven to 400°F (200°C, gas mark 6).

2.   Sieve the flours and baking powder into a mixing bowl
and add the margarine (cut into small pieces).

3.   Rub the margarine into the flour until it feels like fine
breadcrumbs.

4.   Add the sugar and milk and mix to a soft, but not sticky, dough, using a table knife.

5.   Sprinkle flour from a flour dredger onto a pastry board. Turn the dough onto the board and roll it out to a 15 cm circle and then place this on the baking tray with an egg slice.

(If microwaving, go to Stage 2 of the Microwave Method.)

6.   Arrange the peach slices in a circle around the outside edge, with their ends pointing towards the centre, and then

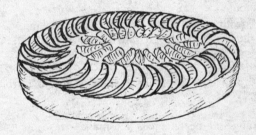

Fig. 35. Arranging peach slices & mandarins

place the mandarin segments in the centre-space in the same way.

7.   Bake for 15-20 minutes until well risen and turning golden brown.

8.   Serve warm or completely cold with orange cream, made by whipping 150 ml double cream and 2 tablespoons of sifted icing sugar together and then folding in 2 teaspoons of finely grated orange zest. OR serve with orange yoghurt –

stir 2 teaspoons of finely grated orange zest into 150ml
Greek yoghurt.

To freeze
Cool, open freeze until solid and then pack in foil and a
plastic bag, seal, label and freeze for up to 3 months.

To serve from frozen
Place the unwrapped pizza on a baking tray, cover with foil
and bake at 375°F (190°C, gas mark 5) for about 20
minutes.

To microwave   *Takes 25 mins. to prepare*
                                        5 mins. to cook

1. Follow Steps 2-5 of the Conventional Cooking Method,
but put the rolled-out dough onto a plate instead of a baking
tray.

2. Microwave on HIGH for 2 minutes. Remove from the
oven.

3. Arrange the peach slices and mandarin segments as in
Stage 6 of the Conventional Cooking Method.

4. Microwave on HIGH for 3 minutes.

Serve warm or completely cold with orange cream or yoghurt
as described in Stage 8 of the Conventional Method.

APPLE OAT CRUMBLE

Cost: ££   *Age: 7+*

A combination of wholemeal flour and oats gives a nutty flavour to this crumble. Cox's eating apples also give an unusual flavour. It can be made more economical if cooking apples are used.

Takes 30 mins. to prepare   *Serves 4-6*
45 mins. to cook

You will need: *Equipment:*

100g wholemeal flour   **scales**
100g hard margarine   **tablespoon**
50g porridge oats   **mixing bowl**
50g soft dark brown sugar   **table knife**
500g Cox's apples (OR   **vegetable knife**
  cooking apples)   **chopping board**
50g soft dark brown sugar   **ovenproof pie dish**
1 teaspoon ground cinnamon   **(1½ litre)**
2 tablespoons water   **teaspoon**
                                      oven gloves

Method

1.   Preheat the oven to 375°F (190°C, gas mark 5).

2.   Make the crumble – put the flour in a mixing bowl. Add the margarine (cut into small pieces) and rub in with your fingertips until the mixture is crumbly. Mix in the oats and 50g of the sugar and then leave on one side.

3.   Peel, core and thinly slice the apples, using a vegetable

knife and chopping board, and put them in the pie dish.
Sprinkle them with the remaining 50g sugar and with the
spice and water.

4.   Spread the crumble mixture over the apples, keeping the
top level.

(If microwaving, go to Stage 2 of the Microwave Method.)

5.   Bake for 40-45 minutes until the topping is golden.

Serve hot with custard or yoghurt.

To freeze
The crumble may be frozen separately in a plastic bag,
uncooked, for up to 4 months. As apples are readily available
all year round it is not necessary to freeze them.

To serve from frozen
The crumble may be sprinkled on top of prepared fruit
straight from the freezer and cooked as above.

To microwave   *Takes 30 mins. to prepare*
                                        16 mins. to cook

1.   Follow steps 2-4 of the Conventional Cooking Method,
but make sure you use a microwave-proof dish.

2.   Microwave on HIGH for 12-14 minutes.

3.   The top may be browned under a preheated grill for 2-3
minutes.

Serve hot with custard or yoghurt.

FRUIT FOOL

Cost: £   *Age: 7+*

This is a quick dessert if you are in a hurry!

Takes 10 mins. to prepare   *Serves 4*
      15 mins. to cook

You will need: *Equipment:*
300ml milk   **measuring jug**
20g semolina   **small saucepan**
20g white sugar   **tablespoon**
300g tin of sharp fruit   **scales**
(rhubarb, gooseberries,   **wooden spoon**
blackberries, raspberries)   **tin opener**
                                    serving dishes

Method

1. Put the milk into a saucepan and warm on a medium heat for 2-3 minutes.

2. Sprinkle the semolina in and stir with a wooden spoon.

3. Cook until it boils and thickens. Add the sugar and cook on a low heat for another 3-4 minutes.

4. Carefully open the tin of fruit *(mind the sharp edges on your fingers!)* and mix into the semolina.

5. Heat for another 1-2 minutes to warm right through.

Pour into individual dishes and serve immediately.

To microwave   *Takes 10 mins. to prepare*
                                13 mins. to cook
                                5 mins. to stand

1. Put the milk, semolina and sugar into a 1 litre glass dish.

2. Microwave on HIGH for about 4 minutes or until the milk boils, stirring once.

3. Stir the pudding again, cover with a lid and cook on HIGH for 2 minutes and then reduce the setting to LOW for a further 7-10 minutes until creamy, stirring 2 or 3 times during cooking.

4. Remove the lid and pour in the tinned fruit. Stir and re-cover and then leave to stand for 5 minutes.

5. Stir again and serve immediately.

MINCE PIES

Cost: £   *Age: 7+*

A sweet shortcrust pastry is used for these special pies for
Christmas and parties.

Takes 25 mins. to prepare   *Makes 12*
        15 mins. to cook

You will need: *Equipment:*
75g soft margarine   **scales**
50g white sugar   **mixing bowl**
1 egg yolk   **table knife**
100g plain white flour   **tablespoon**
50g wholemeal flour   **wooden spoon**
½ teaspoon baking powder   **sieve**
1-2 tablespoons cold water   **teaspoon**
150g mincemeat   **pastry board**
                                    flour dredger
                                    rolling pin
                                    7cm pastry cutter
                                    12-hole bun tray
                                    5-6cm pastry cutter
                                    oven gloves
                                    cooling rack

Method

1.   Preheat the oven to 350°F (180°C, gas mark 4).

2.   Put the margarine and sugar into the mixing bowl and
cream together with a wooden spoon until soft and light.

3.   Beat in the egg yolk and then sieve in the flours and
baking powder and mix them in.

4.   Gradually add enough water to bind it together, adding
about 1 teaspoonful at a time.

5.   Sprinkle flour from a flour dredger onto a pastry board.
Turn the dough onto the board and knead it gently until
smooth and then roll it out fairly thin (about 3mm thick).

6.   Cut out 12 large rounds with the 7cm pastry cutter, and use these to line the bun wells.

7.   Put about ½ tablespoonful of mincemeat into each one.

8.   Gather up and re-roll the remaining pastry and cut 12 lids using the smaller pastry cutter. Make a small slit in the centre of each one with a knife.

9.   Place the lids on top of the mincemeat and press the edges to join the lids and bottoms together.

10. Bake in the centre of the oven for about 15 minutes until golden.

11. Leave the pies in the tin for 5 minutes and then very carefully lift them onto a cooling rack with a knife.

Serve warm or cold. For that special occasion, such as Christmas, serve with Brandy Butter.

To make Brandy Butter
Cream together 50g unsalted butter with 100g sieved icing sugar (with a wooden spoon) and then gradually blend in 2 tablespoonfuls of Brandy (ask an adult first!) or about ½-1 teaspoonful of Brandy essence.

To freeze
Open freeze until solid and then pack into plastic bags or boxes. Seal, label and freeze for up to 3 months.

To serve from frozen
Return them to the bun tray and reheat in a preheated oven at 350°F (180°C, gas mark 4) for 15 minutes, to serve warm. To serve cold – leave uncovered at room temperature for about 1-2 hours.

CHRISTMAS BUNS

Cost: £££   *Age: 7+*

Make large or mini fruity and spicy buns. They are decorated with icing and cherries for that Christmas look.

Takes 40 mins. to prepare   *Makes 12 large*
10 mins. to cook   *or 24 mini buns*

You will need:
225g self-raising flour
125g hard margarine
125g white sugar
½ teaspoon mixed spice
¾ teaspoon ground cinnamon
100g mixed dried fruit
  (currants, sultanas and
  peel)
1 egg, size 4
a little milk
50g icing sugar
6 glacé cherries
angelica

Equipment:
scales
mixing bowl
sieve
tablespoon
2 table knives
teaspoon
fork
small bowl
wooden spoon
baking tray
oven gloves
cooling rack
palette knife

Method

1.   Preheat the oven to 475°F (240°C, gas mark 9).

2.   Sift the flour into a bowl and add the margarine (cut into small pieces). Rub in with your fingertips until the mixture resembles fine breadcrumbs.

3.   Stir in the sugar, spices and mixed fruit.

4.   Break the egg into a small bowl and beat lightly with a fork and then add it to the flour mixture. Mix to a fairly stiff dough with a wodden spoon (a little milk may be needed at this stage).

5.   Place slightly rounded tablespoonfuls of the mixture on a baking tray, leaving space between each one so that it can spread slightly. (For mini buns use heaped teaspoonfuls.)

6.   Bake in the centre of the oven for about 10 minutes, until golden brown. (Mini buns take about 7-8 minutes).

7.   Remove with a palette knife onto a cooling rack.

8.   Meanwhile, make the icing – mix the icing sugar with a little cold water, added *very* gradually, 1-2 teaspoonfuls first

Fig. 36. Stage 5

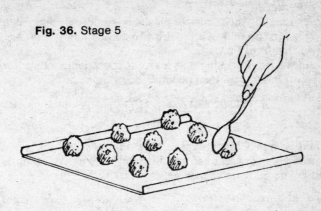

and then drop by drop, until the icing will coat the back of a spoon without running off.

Fig. 37. Coat the back of the spoon with the icing

9. When the buns are cold, spread a little of the icing over the top of each one and then decorate with half a cherry and 2 small pieces of angelica. (Use a quarter cherry for the mini buns.)

To store
These keep very well for 2-3 weeks in an airtight container.

To freeze
Pack into polythene bags or plastic boxes, secure and label.
Freeze for up to 4 months. Best frozen before decorating.
To serve from frozen
Remove from packing and leave at room temperature for
about 2 hours and then decorate as at Stage 8.

CHRISTMAS IGLOO CAKE

Cost: £££   *Age: 7+*

This is a real Christmas cake, on a small scale, which is best
made about 6 weeks before Christmas. Use a pudding basin
to create an igloo-shaped cake!

Takes 1 hour 20 mins.   *Serve 6-8*
plus cooling and drying time if possible
         45 mins. to cook

You will need: *Equipment:*
oil for greasing   pastry brush
50g soft margarine OR butter   600ml pudding basin
50g soft dark brown sugar   scales
1 dessertspoon black treacle   2 table knives
1 egg, size 4   mixing bowl
75g plain white flour   tablespoon
½ teaspoon mixed spice   wooden spoon
1 dessertspoon orange juice   2 dessertspoons
   OR milk   small bowl
2 teaspoons rum OR brandy   fork
   essence   sieve
25g cherries   2 teaspoons
150g mixed dried fruit   oven gloves
                                    baking tray
For the decoration: wooden cocktail
1-2 tablespoons apricot jam   stick
125g white marzipan   cooling rack
1 egg white   small saucepan
few drops glycerine   pastry board
225g icing sugar   rolling pin
                                    15cm cake board or
                                       plate

Method

1. Preheat the oven to 325°F (170°C, gas mark 3). Grease the pudding basin.

2. Put the margarine or butter into a mixing bowl with the sugar and beat well with a wooden spoon until soft and creamy. Mix in the treacle.

3. Break the egg into a small bowl and beat with a fork. Add a little of the egg to the butter and sugar and beat in well, then sieve and stir in some of the flour and spice. Repeat this process, alternately adding the egg and flour until it's all been added.

4. Mix in the orange juice or milk, and the essence.

5. Cut the cherries into quarters and add to the mixture.

6. Finally add the mixed fruit and combine it all together well.

7. Place the mixture in the basin and make it level. Stand the basin on a baking tray and bake in the centre of the oven for 40-45 minutes. Test with a wooden cocktail stick inserted into the centre of the cake; it should come out clean when it's cooked.

8. Leave in the basin for 5 minutes and then turn it out, upside-down, onto a wire cooling rack and leave until cold.

If the cake has been made well in advance, it should be left at this stage to mature, wrapped in foil and kept in a cool place until about 1 week before it is required, and then continue:

9. Put the jam into a saucepan and warm gently over a low heat to melt it and then brush it all over the cake, keeping the cake upside-down.

10. Knead the marzipan until smooth on a pastry board, and then roll it out fairly thinly into a circle 25cm in diameter. Carefully lift it by folding about half of it over the rolling pin, and place it over the cake, taking care to lay it evenly and

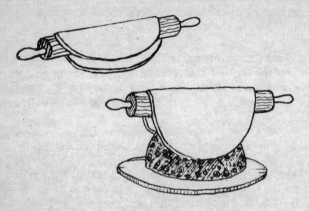

Fig. 38. Lifting marzipan with rolling pin and placing on cake

then mould it over the cake with your hands. Neaten the bottom edges by trimming with a knife.

The cake should be left again for a few days at this stage for the marzipan to dry out before icing. However, white marzipan has been used instead of the usual yellow so that the oils in it are less likely to show through to the icing if you haven't enough time to leave it to dry.

11. Make the icing – put the egg white and glycerine into a bowl and lightly break it up with a fork. Sieve the icing sugar in and mix it to a smooth and shiny consistency with a wooden spoon. It should be thick enough to stand up in peaks when pulled up with the back of the spoon.

12. Put a small blob of icing in the centre of the cake board and place the cake on this to secure it in place. Put all the icing on top of the cake and, using a knife, gradually spread it evenly down the sides and over the top. Then, using the back of a teaspoon, "rough ice" it by pulling the icing up into peaks. Allow to dry for at least 24 hours.

Fig. 39. Rough icing

To store

This cake will keep very well in an airtight tin for several weeks.

To freeze

After Stage 8, before decorating: wrap in foil and a plastic bag, seal, label and freeze for up to 6 months.

To serve from frozen

Unwrap and thaw at room temperature for 4 hours and then proceed from Stage 9 to decorate.

ALPHABET COOKIES

Cost: £   *Age:* 7+

Have fun making your own initials, or how about one for
Mum and Dad, even G for Grandad or Grannie – or, what
about your Valentine! Then put some chocolate on them –
hmm!

Takes 45 mins. to prepare   *Makes several*
plus cooling time
     10 mins. to cook

You will need: *Equipment:*

100g soft margarine   scales
100g soft brown sugar   mixing bowl
1 egg, size 4   tablespoon
150g wholemeal flour   2 table knives
50g porridge oats   wooden spoon
75g coconut   pastry board
75-100g cooking chocolate   flour dredger
                                 rolling pin
                                 2 baking trays
                                 egg slice
                                 oven gloves
                                 cooling rack
                                 basin
                                 small saucepan

Method
1.   Preheat the oven to 350°F (180°C, gas mark 4).

2.   Put the margarine and sugar into a mixing bowl and beat
well with a wooden spoon until light and fluffy. Add the egg
and beat in.

3.   Add the dry ingredients (except the chocolate) and mix
well until they are all combined to form a firm dough.

4. Gather the dough into a ball. Sprinkle flour from a flour dredger onto a pastry board. Then knead the dough gently on the board until smooth.

5. Roll out to about 3mm thick and, using a knife, cut out your chosen letters making them about 10cm high. (It may be easier to make patterns from stiff paper to cut around.)

6. Carefully lift them onto the baking trays, using an egg slice.

7. Bake just above the centre of the oven for 7-10 minutes, until golden brown.

8. Leave on the trays for 3-4 minutes to harden a little before lifting (with the egg slice again) onto a cooling rack.

9. Meanwhile, break the chocolate into small pieces and put into a small basin fitted over a pan of hot water on a low heat so that it melts (see page 70) and then use it to decorate the biscuits with dribbled zig-zags, wiggly lines or just spread all over the tops.

Fig. 40. Final cookie shape

To store
These will keep well in an airtight tin for about 1-2 weeks.

CHRISTMAS STARS

Cost: £   *Age: 7+*

Better make a big batch of these irresistible biscuits – they
won't stay in the tin for long!

Takes 45 mins. to prepare   *Makes about 24*
plus cooling time
7 mins. to cook

You will need: *Equipment:*
100g soft margarine   **scales**
50g white sugar   **mixing bowl**
1 egg, size 4   **2 tablespoons**
1 orange   **2 table knives**
150g plain white flour   **wooden spoon**
50g rice flour   **grater**
2 teaspoons mixed spice   **orange squeezer**
75g mixed peel   **sieve**
25g currants   **pastry board**
50g icing sugar   **flour dredger**
                                      rolling pin
                                      star-shaped biscuit
                                         cutter
                                      palette knife/egg
                                         slice
                                      2 baking trays
                                      oven gloves
                                      cooling rack
                                      small bowl

Method

1. Preheat the oven to 375°F (190°C, gas mark 5).

2. Cream the margarine and sugar together with a wooden spoon in a large mixing bowl and then add the egg and beat well.

3. Carefully grate the zest of the orange and add to the mixture. Cut the orange in half, squeeze the juice and add one tablespoonful of the juice to the ingredients in the mixing bowl.

4. Sieve the flours into the bowl. Add the spice, mixed peel and currants and mix together to make a firm dough.

5. Form the dough into a ball. Sprinkle flour from a flour dredger onto a pastry board. Knead the dough gently on the board until smooth. Roll it out as thinly as the fruit will allow and, using a star-shaped cutter, cut out the biscuits, gathering up and re-rolling the off-cuts each time and cutting more biscuits until all the dough is used.

6. Place the biscuits onto the baking trays with a palette knife or egg slice and cook just above the centre of the oven for 6-7 minutes, until just golden.

7. Transfer to a wire cooling rack (with a palette knife) and leave to cool.

8. Meanwhile, make the icing – mix a little warm water with the icing sugar in a small bowl, adding it drop by drop, to get a thick but slightly runny consistency.

9. Run the icing over the biscuits in a zig-zag pattern using a teaspoon, as in fig 41 overleaf.

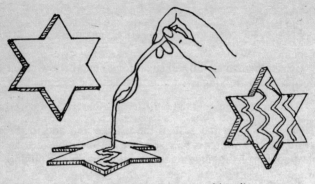

Fig. 41. Running icing over biscuits
in zig zags

To store
These will keep for 1-2 weeks in an airtight tin.

FONDANTS

Cost: £   *Age: 7+*

A friend gave me this recipe and I regularly make it for
Christmas presents, together with other sweets from this
book.

Takes 1 hour to prepare   *Makes lots!*

You will need:
1 egg white
225-275g icing sugar
2 teaspoons glycerine OR
    25g soft margarine
various flavourings and
    colours

Equipment:
mixing bowl
fork
scales
tablespoon
sieve
wooden spoon
teaspoon
table knife
pastry board
rolling pin
shaped sweet cutters
baking tray

Method

1.   Put the egg white into a large mixing bowl and beat with a fork to break it up and then gradually sieve in the icing sugar and beat it in with a wooden spoon. Add the glycerine OR margarine when about half of the icing has been added. Beat well until smooth.

2.   Add the remaining half of the icing sugar and beat well again. Then knead it with your hands to make a stiff mixture (it should not stick to the hands).

3.   Divide the mixture into 2, 3 or 4 pieces and then flavour and colour each piece as liked, adding both the flavouring and colouring drop by drop from a teaspoon – remember these are concentrated – more can be added but not taken away!

For example: lemon flavour, yellow colour
strawberry flavour, pink colour
peppermint flavour, green colour (or
leave white)
orange flavour, orange colour

4.   Sprinkle each piece with a little icing sugar to stop it sticking to the board and rolling pin. Then roll each piece out

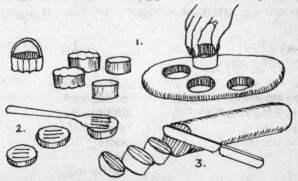

Fig. 42. Cutting shapes. Pressing out with a fork. Cutting into slices.

separately to about ½cm thick. Cut out the shapes with sweet cutters; or alternatively, shape the mixture into small balls and press out with a fork: or roll into a long sausage shape and cut off into 1cm slices.

5.   Leave the sweets on a baking tray to dry out for about 24 hours.

To store
These will keep for 3-4 weeks in an airtight container such as a glass jar, but must be well dried out first.

To make a present
Make a selection of shapes and colours and pack in a small box, or on a foil tray with a doyley placed inside. Cover with cling film and decorate with coloured paper or ribbons.

CHOCOLATE COCONUT ICE

Cost: ££   *Age: 7+*

This is a recipe given to me by my father and is another favourite for giving as Christmas presents. It is very moreish!

Takes 30 mins. to prepare   *Makes about 450g*
plus setting time

You will need: *Equipment:*
196g tin condensed milk   **mixing bowl**
150g icing sugar   **tin opener**
25g cocoa   **table knife**
100g coconut   **scales**
                                  sieve
                                  tablespoon
                                  wooden spoon
                                  dish or tin
                                     (16cm square)

Method

1. Carefully open the tin of milk *(remember to mind the sharp edges!)* and pour the milk into a mixing bowl, scraping the tin clean with a knife.

2. Sieve the icing sugar into the bowl and add the cocoa. Mix it together with a wooden spoon, slowly at first (the icing and cocoa will "fly" all over if it's not done carefully) and then more briskly so that it combines well.

3. Add the coconut and work it well in (this will get stiff).

4. Put the mixture into a dish or tin and leave it to dry out away from direct heat. (A warm kitchen will do.)

5. Cut into squares of about 2 cm when almost set. This will take roughly 4 hours, depending upon the temperature of your kitchen.

To store
This will keep for 3-4 weeks in an airtight container.

To make a present
Make a selection of sweets from this book and assemble them in a clean, empty jar. Cover the lid with a scrap of pretty material or coloured paper and doyley.

FRUIT AND NUT CLUSTERS

Cost: £   *Age: 7+*

This is another very easy and quick sweet recipe.

Takes 30 mins. to prepare   *Makes 12*

You will need:
1 Mars bar
50g raisins
1 dessertspoon milk
15g chopped nuts
15g crispie breakfast cereal

Equipment:
chopping board
vegetable knife
basin
small saucepan
dessertspoon
scales
tablespoon
table knife
teaspoon
paper sweet cases

Method
1. Chop the Mars bar (using a vegetable knife and chopping board). Put it into a basin fitted over a pan of hot water on a low heat so that it melts (see page 21).

2. Chop the raisins and add them with all the other ingredients to the melted chocolate. Mix it well so that the ingredients are evenly coated.

3. Pile a teaspoonful of the mixture into each paper sweet case and then leave to set.

To store
In an airtight container for 1-2 weeks.

SPRING

The Season for
Fêtes, Fairs,
Mothers' Day and Easter

CHEESE AND PINEAPPLE SALAD

Cost: ££   *Age:* 7+

This vegetarian dish is made with a low fat cheese.

Takes 40 mins. to prepare   *Serves 2*

You will need: *Equipment:*
½ head of lettuce   colander
50g dates   serving dish
2 pineapple rings (tinned) vegetable knife
  plus juice   chopping board
200g cottage cheese   small bowl
¼ cucumber   tin opener

Method

1. Wash the lettuce and drain well in a colander and then tear into small pieces and put on a serving dish.

2. Chop the dates roughly on a chopping board with a vegetable knife and put into a small bowl.

3. Open the tin of pineapple carefully. Drain the pineapple and chop into small pieces and add to the dates.

4. Put the cheese into the bowl and mix altogether with 1-2 tablespoons of the pineapple juice.

5. Slice the cucumber thinly.

6. Assemble the salad – pile the cheese mixture on top of the lettuce and surround with the cucumber.

Serve with fresh wholemeal bread.

Fig. 43. Assembling the salad

BUTTERFLY EGGS

Cost: ££   *Age: 7+*

Choose which you like best – cheesy eggs or fishy eggs.

Takes 45 mins. to prepare   *Serves 3*
         10 mins. to cook

CHEESY BUTTERFLY EGGS

You will need:	*Equipment:*
3 eggs, size 3	saucepan
3 small chipolatas	kitchen scissors
1 box cress	chopping board
75g grated cheese	colander
1 dessertspoon mayonnaise	vegetable knife
1 tablespoon fresh parsley	small bowl
carrot to decorate	grater
	dessertspoon
	tablespoon
	fork
	serving plate

Method

1.   Turn the grill on to a medium heat. Meanwhile, hard boil the eggs – place the eggs in a saucepan and cover with cold water. Put on a high heat and bring to the boil and then reduce the heat and simmer for 10 minutes.

2.   Place the chipolatas on the grill pan and cook under the preheated grill for about 10 minutes, turning several times with a fork, until brown all over. Leave on one side to cool.

3.   Cut the cress with kitchen scissors, put into a colander and wash under cold running water and then drain well.

4.   Cool the eggs in cold water and then shell them.

5.   Cut the eggs in half lengthways, carefully take out the yolks with a teaspoon and place them in a small bowl with the cheese, mayonnaise and parsley. Mix together with a fork.

6. Pile the mixture back into the white cases, taking care not to break them.

7. Assemble the butterflies on a serving plate. First, put the cress on the plate and then put one chipolata with one half egg

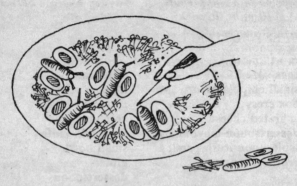

Fig. 44. Assembling the butterflies

on either side of it for the wings. Cut matchstick-like strips of carrot and place in the ends of the chipolatas for antennae by making a small slit in the chipolatas with a sharp knife. Repeat with the remaining chipolatas and eggs.

FISHY BUTTERFLY EGGS

You will need:
½ 120g can sardines and
1 teaspoon lemon juice
plus the other ingredients but without the cheese

Use the same method as above, replacing the cheese with sardines and lemon juice and mixing these with the egg yolks, mayonnaise and parsley. Serve immediately.

SURPRISE SAUSAGE ROLLS

Cost: £   *Age: 7+*

These rolls are made with bread instead of pastry.

Takes 30 mins. to prepare   *Makes 8*
25 mins. to cook

You will need: *Equipment:*

4 slices of bread   **table knife**
50g cheese, Cheddar or   **pastry board**
Leicester   **rolling pin**
25g soft margarine   **scales**
1 teaspoon dry mustard   **grater**
1 teaspoon tomato purée OR   **small bowl**
ketchup   **teaspoon**
4 chipolata sausages   **fork**
                                           cocktail sticks
                                           baking tray
                                           oven gloves

Method
1.   Preheat the oven to 400°F (200°C, gas mark 6).

2.   Cut the crusts off the bread, taking care not to waste any
bread, and then roll the slices with a rolling pin so that they
become firm.

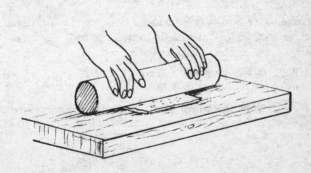

Fig. 45. Rolling the slices to become firm

3. Carefully grate the cheese into a small bowl *(mind your fingers!)*.

4. Add the margarine, mustard and tomato purée or ketchup to the cheese and mix together with a fork.

5. Spread equal amounts of the cheese mixture over each slice of bread, then put a sausage on each one and roll round,

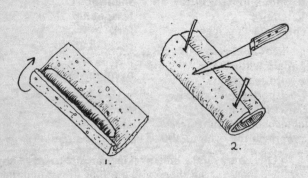

Fig. 46. Making the sausage rolls

completely enclosing the sausage. Secure with a cocktail stick at each end. Cut in half to make 2 rolls from each piece.

6. Place on a baking tray and cook for 20-25 minutes until golden brown.

Best eaten while still warm. Not suitable for reheating – they become hard.

SAVOURY TART

Cost: £   *Age: 7+*

This is good for a packed lunch or picnic; it goes well with a salad too.

Takes 45 mins. to prepare   *Serves 4-6*
*   30 mins. to cook*

You will need: *Equipment:*

50g Cheddar cheese   **scales**
75g plain white flour   **grater**
40g hard margarine   **tablespoon**
3-4 teaspoons cold water   **mixing bowl**
1-2 slices lean ham   **sieve**
1 tablespoon onion, finely   **table knife**
**   chopped**   **pastry board**
1 egg, size 4   **flour dredger**
75ml milk   **rolling pin**
pinch of salt and pepper   **18cm flan tin**
                                        **   2½cm deep**
                                        fork
                                        oven gloves
                                        baking tray
                                        chopping board
                                        vegetable knife
                                        measuring jug

Method
1.   Preheat the oven to 400°F (200°C, gas mark 6).

2.   Grate the cheese on a fine grater *(mind your fingers!)*.

3.   Sieve the flour into a bowl, add the margarine (cut into small pieces) and rub in with your fingertips until it resembles fine breadcrumbs.

4. Stir in 40g of the cheese and bind together with a little water to form a firm dough.

5. Sprinkle a pastry board with flour from a flour dredger. Roll out the pastry onto the board and line the flan tin with it. Prick the base all over with a fork and bake blind for 5-10 minutes until just beginning to brown. Remove from the oven and place on a baking tray.

6. Meanwhile, chop the ham into pieces roughly 1cm square. Chop or grate the onion finely *(mind your fingers on sharp tools!)*.

7. Put the ham and onion into the cooked pastry case.

8. Mix the egg and milk together with a fork and season with a pinch or two of salt and pepper. Pour it over the ham and onion and then sprinkle the remaining cheese on the top.

(If microwaving, go to Stage 6 of the Microwave Method.)

9. Bake for about 15-20 minutes until the custard is set and lightly browned.

Serve warm or cold.

To freeze
Cool, open freeze until solid and pack in a plastic bag or box. Seal, label and freeze for up to 2 months.

To serve from frozen
Remove from bag and thaw at room temperature for about 2 hours or reheat from frozen for about 15-20 minutes at 350°F (180°C, gas mark 4).

To microwave   *Takes 45 mins. to prepare*
                                                17 mins. to cook
                                                and standing time

1.   Grate the cheese on a fine grater *(mind your fingers!).*

2.   Sieve the flour into a bowl, add the margarine (cut into small pieces) and rub in with your fingertips until it resembles fine breadcrumbs.

3.   Stir in 40g of the cheese and bind together with 1 tablespoon of water to form a firm dough.

4.   Sprinkle a pastry board with flour from a flour dredger. Roll out the pastry onto the board and line the flan dish with it. Place a piece of absorbent kitchen paper over the base, gently pressing into the corners between the base and sides of the dish. Microwave on HIGH for 5 minutes. Remove the paper.

5.   Follow Stages 6-8 of the Conventional Cooking Method.

6.   Cook on DEFROST for 12 minutes and then allow to stand for a few minutes.

Serve warm or cold.

CORNISH PASTIES

Cost: £   *Age: 10+*

This is my variation of a very well known favourite old recipe.

Takes 1 hour 10 mins. to prepare   *Makes 4*
45 mins. to cook

You will need:

225g plain white flour
50g hard margarine
50g white cooking fat
approx. 2 tablespoons cold
  water
225g lean minced beef
225g potatoes
50g onion
2 tablespoons tomato ketchup
milk to glaze

Equipment:

2 mixing bowls
scales
tablespoon
sieve
table knife
fork
potato peeler
vegetable knife
chopping board
pastry board
flour dredger
rolling pin
pastry brush
2 baking trays
oven gloves

Method

1. Preheat the oven to 350°F (180°C, gas mark 4).

2. Make the pastry – sieve the flour into a large mixing bowl and add both the fats (cut into small pieces). Rub in until crumbly, and then bind together with the cold water, using a knife, and then knead it lightly into a ball, leaving the bowl clean. Leave on one side.

3. Put the meat into a large bowl and break it up with a fork.

4. Peel the potatoes, then wash them and chop into small thin pieces. Add to the meat.

5. Peel the onion and chop it finely. Add to the meat.

6.   Put the tomato ketchup in the bowl with the meat and vegetables and mix well together.

7.   Sprinkle flour from a flour dredger onto a pastry board. Cut the pastry into 4 equal pieces and on the board roll out one piece fairly thinly to approximately the size of a small teaplate.

8.   Divide the meat mixture into 4 equal parts and put one part in the centre of the pastry round.

9.   Dampen the edges of the pastry with a little water and then bring them up to join at the centre, covering the filling. Pinch the edges together to seal them and then flute the edge

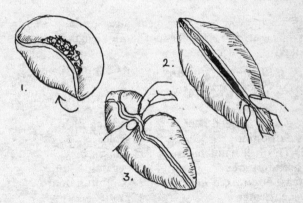

Fig. 47. (1) Arranging the pastry over the filling
            (2) Pinching the edges to seal
            (3) Fluting the edges

with your fingers. Repeat with the remaining 3 pieces of pastry and portions of meat.

10.   Place them onto the baking trays and brush with a little milk to glaze.

11.   Bake in the centre of the oven for 30 minutes and then reduce the heat to 300°F (150°C, gas mark 2) for a further 15 minutes.

Serve hot with vegetables or cold for a packed lunch, or with
a salad.

To freeze
Cool, pack into plastic bags or boxes. Seal, label and freeze
for up to 4 months.

To serve from frozen
Remove the wrapping, place on a baking tray, cover with foil
and reheat for about 30-45 minutes at 400°F (200°C, gas
mark 6).

SPAGHETTI NESTS

Cost: £££   *Age:* 7+

This is a fun way of serving meatballs. Spaghetti is easier to
serve and eat if it is broken into shorter lengths before being
cooked.

Takes 40 mins. to prepare   *Serves 3-4*
35 mins. to cook

You will need:
225g lean minced beef
1 small onion
25g (1 slice) wholemeal
   breadcrumbs
1 teaspoon mixed herbs
½ egg, beaten
1-2 tablespoons vegetable
   oil
300ml beef stock (made with
   stock cube)
225g spaghetti
1 heaped teaspoon cornflour
2 tablespoons tomato purée
Parmesan or grated Cheddar

Equipment:
serving dish
scales
mixing bowl
vegetable knife
chopping board
grater
teaspoon
2 small bowls
fork
tablespoon
plate
frying pan
measuring jug
large saucepan with
   lid
oven gloves
wooden spoon
colander

Method

1.   Set the oven to its lowest temperature and put in the serving dish to warm it. Put the beef into a large bowl.

2.   Peel, wash and finely chop the onion and mix with the beef.

3.   To make breadcrumbs, cut off the crusts and then grate the bread into the meat and onion *(mind you don't grate your fingers!)*.

4.   Add the herbs. Put the egg in a small bowl and beat it with a fork. Add the egg to the mixture and bind it altogether.

5.   Wet your hands with cold water and then take a tablespoonful of the mixture and shape it into a ball with your wet hands and then place it on a plate. Repeat with the rest of the mixture so that you make about 8 balls.

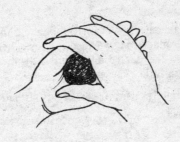

Fig. 48. Shaping mixture into a ball

(If microwaving, go to Stage 2 of the Microwave Method.)

6.   Heat the oil in a frying pan over a medium heat for 1-2 minutes and then carefully place the meatballs in the pan without touching each other. Fry until browned all over, turning several times.

7.   Crumble the stock cube into a measuring jug, add 300ml of boiling water and stir with a spoon so that the cube dissolves. Add the stock and simmer gently for 15 minutes.

8. Meanwhile, break the spaghetti into shorter lengths (roughly 10cm is quite manageable). Half fill the saucepan with cold water and put on a high heat so that it boils. Carefully put the spaghetti into the pan *(remember steam can scald!)*. Cover with the lid and simmer for 10 minutes until tender.

9. At the end of the meatballs' cooking time, put them onto the warm dish to keep warm. *Remember to use oven gloves to handle the warm dish.* Leave the stock in the frying pan.

10. Put the cornflour into a small bowl and blend with 2-3 teaspoons of cold water until smooth and then add to the reduced meatball stock, together with the tomato purée. Bring to the boil, stirring with a wooden spoon until slightly thickened.

11. Return the meatballs to the sauce for 3-4 minutes to heat through.

12. Assemble the nests – strain the spaghetti thoroughly in a colander and place on warmed plates, then spoon the meatballs onto the centre and pour the sauce over them. Sprinkle with a little cheese.

Serve immediately with fresh crusty bread and a side salad.

To freeze
Cool the meatballs in the sauce and pour into a waxed or plastic box, label and freeze for up to 4 months. Spaghetti is best not frozen.

To serve from frozen
Pour into a saucepan and heat very gently, over a low heat, stirring from time to time.

To microwave   *Takes 40 mins. to prepare*
                                         24 mins. to cook

1. Follow Stages 1-5 of the Conventional Cooking Method.

2. Put the meatballs into a microwave-proof dish, cover and cook on HIGH for 7 minutes.

3. To make the sauce, put the cornflour into a jug and blend with about 1 tablespoonful of the stock until smooth. Add the rest of the stock and the purée and microwave on HIGH for 5 minutes, stirring every minute until thickened.

4. Pour the sauce over the meatballs and microwave on HIGH for 3 minutes to warm through and leave to stand while the spaghetti cooks.

5. Put the spaghetti, broken into lengths of about 10cm, into a large bowl and pour boiling water over to cover it. Stir, cover and microwave for 9¼ minutes on HIGH.

6. Strain the spaghetti in a colander and then place on warm plates, spoon the meatballs onto the centre and pour the sauce over them. Sprinkle with a little cheese.

Serve immediately with fresh crusty bread and a side salad.

QUICK PIZZA

Cost: £   *Age: 7+*

This quick tasty pizza has a scone-type base made with wholemeal flour.

Takes 30 mins. to prepare   *Serves 2*
*   20 mins. to cook*

You will need: *Equipment:*

100g wholemeal flour   **scales**
1 teaspoon baking powder   **mixing bowl**
25g hard margarine   **tablespoon**
6 tablespoons milk   **teaspoon**
1 tinned tomato OR   **table knife**
** 1 tablespoon tomato purée**   **pastry board**
½ small onion   **flour dredger**
¼ teaspoon dried basil   **rolling pin**
40g Cheddar cheese   **baking tray**
1-2 slices salami   **egg slice**
1-2 pilchards   **tin opener**
1-2 slices green pepper   **chopping board**
                                      vegetable knife
                                      grater
                                      oven gloves

Method
1.   Preheat the oven to 425°F (220°C, gas mark 7).

2.   Put the flour and baking powder into a bowl, add the margarine (cut into small pieces) and rub in with your fingertips until crumbly.

3.   Add the milk and bind together to form a soft dough.

4.   Sprinkle flour from a flour dredger onto a pastry board. Turn the dough onto the board and knead it until smooth. Roll out into a circle about 15 cm in diameter and lift it onto a baking tray with an egg slice.

(If microwaving, go to Stage 2 of the Microwave Method.)

5.   Chop the tinned tomato. Spread 1-2 teaspoons of tomato juice from the tin and the chopped tomato on the base (or spread the tomato purée if preferred).

6.   Peel, wash and finely chop the onion and sprinkle it over the tomato. Then sprinkle the herbs over it.

Fig. 49. Splitting the pilchard and removing the bones

7.   Grate the cheese on a coarse grater *(mind your fingers!)* and then sprinkle it on top of the onion.

8.   Cut the salami into bite-sized pieces and dot them about over the cheese.

9.   Carefully split the pilchard open lengthways and remove the bones. Then cut the fish into pieces and place it, skin side uppermost, on top of the cheese, between the salami pieces.

10.   Chop the pepper and dot it all over the pizza, skin side uppermost.

(If microwaving, go to Stage 4 of the Microwave Method.)

11.   Bake just above the centre of the oven for 15-20 minutes.

Serve warm with a fresh green salad.

To freeze
Cool, open freeze until solid and pack in foil and a plastic bag, seal, label and freeze for up to 3 months.

To serve from frozen
Place the unwrapped frozen pizza on a baking tray and bake at 400°F (200°C, gas mark 6) for about 20 minutes. Cover with foil if the top begins to dry up too much.

To microwave   *Takes 30 mins. to prepare*
                                                     9 mins. to cook

1.   Follow Stages 2-4 of the Conventional Cooking Method, but put the pastry onto a plate rather than a baking tray.

2.   Microwave on HIGH for 3 minutes. Remove from the oven and assemble the topping.

3.   Follow Stages 5-10 of the Conventional Cooking Method.

4.   Microwave on HIGH for 4 minutes and then flash under a preheated grill to brown for 1-2 minutes.

Serve hot.

HOT DREAMY TRIFLE

Cost: £   *Age: 7+*

Use up any cake off-cuts or stale cake in this quick dish.

Takes 20 mins. to prepare   *Serves 4*
*   25 mins. to cook*

You will need: *Equipment:*

4 slices Swiss roll OR   **0.75 litre serving**
  stale cake   **dish**
2 tablespoons red jam if   **table knife**
  using stale cake   **tablespoon**
300g tin blackberries, rasp- **tin opener**
  berries OR strawberries **small saucepan**
1 rounded tablespoon blanc- **wooden spoon**
  mange powder, strawberry **oven gloves**
    OR raspberry
1 tablespoon sugar
300ml milk
10-12 marshmallows

Method

1.   Preheat the oven to 300°F (150°C, gas mark 2).

2.   Cut up the Swiss roll and place it in the dish. If using stale cake or off-cuts, break it up into small pieces, place in the dish and spread the jam over the top.

3.   Open the tin of fruit *(carefully!)* and pour the contents over the sponge base to soak up the juice.

4.   Put the blancmange powder and sugar into a small saucepan and blend with 2 tablespoonfuls of the milk until smooth. Stir in the rest of the milk.

(If microwaving, go to Stage 2 of the Microwave Method.)

5.   Place the saucepan over a fairly high heat and bring to the boil, stirring all the time with a wooden spoon, until thickened.

6.   Pour it over the sponge and fruit and then gently mix them together.

7. Place in the oven for about 10-15 minutes until warmed through. Meanwhile, preheat the grill to medium-hot.

8. Carefully put the marshmallows on the top of the trifle *(remember the dish will be hot)* and then put under the hot grill for 2-3 minutes until beginning to turn golden and melt slightly.

Serve immediately.

To microwave   *Takes 20 mins. to prepare*
                                      12 mins. to cook

1. Follow Stages 2-4 of the Conventional Cooking Method, but remember to use a microwave-proof dish.

2. Microwave on HIGH for 4-5 minutes, stirring every 2 minutes, until thickened.

3. Pour it over the sponge and fruit and then gently mix together.

4. Microwave for about 4 minutes on HIGH until warmed through.

5. Preheat the grill to medium-hot.

6. Put the marshmallows on the top of the trifle and then put it under the hot grill for 2-3 minutes until it is just beginning to turn golden and melt slightly.

Serve immediately.

SAUCER PANCAKES

Cost: £   *Age: 7+*

These mini oven-cooked pancakes are thicker and creamier than the usual frying pan ones. They're delicious served with a fruit purée, syrup, jam or lemon or orange juice and a sprinkling of sugar.

Takes 25 mins. to prepare   *Serves 4*
15 mins. to cook

You will need: *Equipment:*
oil for greasing   **8 saucers or 10cm**
50g soft margarine   **individual tins**
50g white sugar   **pastry brush**
2 eggs, size 4   **baking trays**
75g plain white flour   **scales**
150ml milk   **mixing bowl**
filling to taste (see note   **table knife**
  above)   **tablespoon**
                                        wooden spoon
                                        sieve
                                        measuring jug
                                        serving dishes

Method

1.   Preheat the oven to 425°F (220°C, gas mark 7). Grease the saucers or tins with the oil, place them on baking trays and put them on the oven hob so that they get warm.

2.   Put the margarine and sugar into a mixing bowl and beat together with a wooden spoon until creamy.

3.   Beat in the eggs, one at a time, adding a little sieved flour with each one.

4.   Sieve and beat in the remaining flour.

5.   Gradually mix in the milk, mixing well, making a fairly thin batter.

6.   Put 2½-3 tablespoonfuls of the mixture into each saucer.

7.   Bake near the top of the oven for 10-15 minutes until risen and golden.

Serve immediately with the flavouring of your choice.

To freeze

Turn the cooked pancakes out of the saucers and pile them up with a layer of greaseproof paper between each one. Put them into a plastic bag, seal, label and freeze for up to 1 month.

To serve from frozen
Remove from the bag, separate, place on a baking tray and
reheat at 400°F (200°C, gas mark 6) for 5-10 minutes, and
then serve as above.

HOT CROSS BUNS

Cost: £   *Age: 7+*

An old favourite for Easter, this is a quick and easy
method.

*Takes 1 hour 15 mins. to prepare   Makes 8 buns
               15 mins. to cook*

You will need: *Equipment:*
oil for greasing   baking tray
275g white bread mix   pastry brush
25g white sugar   mixing bowl
½ teaspoon mixed spice   scales
½ teaspoon ground cinnamon   tablespoon
50g dried fruit   teaspoon
200ml hand-hot water   measuring jug
½ beaten egg   table knife
                             pastry board
                             flour dredger
                             clean tea towel
                             sharp knife
                             small bowl
                             fork

Method
1.   Grease the baking tray.

2.   Put the bread mix in a warm, large mixing bowl, add the
sugar, spices and fruit and combine together.

3.   Add the water and mix well together with a knife until all
the flour is absorbed.

4.   Sprinkle flour from a flour dredger onto a pastry board.
Turn the dough onto the board and knead it firmly for
5 minutes until it is smooth and elastic.

5. Divide the dough into 8 equal pieces and shape each one into a round, slightly flattened ball-shape.

(If microwaving, go to Stage 2 of the Microwave Method.)

6. Place on the greased baking tray, leaving space between each one for rising.

7. Wet the tea towel in warm water and wring out tightly and then put over the bread rolls to cover them. Leave in a warm place to rise to double their size (about 35-55 minutes).

8. Preheat the oven while they are rising, to 450°F (230°C, gas mark 8).

9. Check that the buns have risen to double their size, remove the tea towel and make cuts with a sharp knife, just cutting through the surface of the dough, to make a cross on each bun.

10. Beat the egg in a small bowl with a fork. Brush over the buns with the beaten egg to glaze and bake for 10-15 minutes. To test whether a bun is cooked, carefully lift it with a cloth, hold it upside-down and tap it on the bottom. It is cooked when it sounds hollow.

11. Cool on a wire rack.

Serve with butter, warm or cold.

To freeze
Cool, pack in plastic bags, seal, label and freeze for up to 4 months.

To serve from frozen
Unwrap and place on a baking tray covered loosely with foil and reheat at 350°F (180°C, gas mark 4) for about 20 minutes.

To microwave   *Takes 50 mins. to prepare*
                                        6 mins to cook

1. Follow Stages 2-5 of the Conventional Cooking Method.

2. Place 4 buns on a lightly floured plate and microwave on HIGH for 20 *seconds* and then leave to stand for 5-10 minutes. While they are standing, do the same with the other 4 buns. Repeat until all 8 are well risen to double their original size.

3. Make cuts with a sharp knife, just cutting through the surface of the dough, to make a cross on each bun.

4. Cook on HIGH for 2¾ minutes. This will give a soft textured result without browning.

These buns may be browned under a preheated grill if desired.

BANANA ROLLS

Cost: ££   *Age: 7+*

Soft spicy banana inside a crisp crumbly pastry. Use bought puff pastry for these to save time in preparation.

Takes 1 hour to defrost the pastry   *Serves 4*
*   45 mins. to prepare*
*   15 mins. to cook*

You will need: *Equipment:*
225g frozen puff pastry,   **pastry board**
    defrosted   **flour dredger**
1 lemon   **rolling pin**
1 rounded tablespoon sugar   **ruler**
1 teaspoon cinnamon   **grater**
2 medium-sized firm bananas   **2 small bowls**
milk to glaze   **tablespoon**
                                          teaspoon
                                          lemon squeezer
                                          table knife
                                          fork
                                          baking tray
                                          pastry brush
                                          egg slice
                                          oven gloves

Method

1.   Leave the pastry to defrost in a warm kitchen for about 1 hour before you want to use it.

2.   Preheat the oven to 425°F (220°C, gas mark 7).

3.   Sprinkle flour from a flour dredger onto a pastry board. Roll out the defrosted pastry onto the board to about 26cm square, and leave to rest.

4.   Meanwhile, grate the zest from the lemon and mix it with the sugar and spice in a small bowl.

5.   Squeeze the lemon juice into a separate small bowl and put to one side.

6.   Cut the pastry into 4 equal pieces.

7.   Peel and cut across the bananas into halves and toss immediately in the lemon juice to prevent them turning brown.

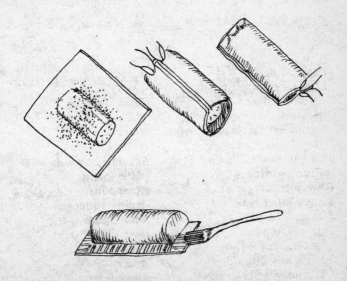

Fig. 50. Wrapping the pastry around the banana

8. Put one piece of banana on each piece of pastry and sprinkle over 1 heaped teaspoon of the sugar and spice mix.

9. Brush the edges of the pastry with water and wrap over the banana to cover completely, bringing the two long sides over to meet at the top, pinching them together to seal and then pinch the ends together to seal also. Lay the roll down with the sealed edges at the base and press a fork on the edges to give a decorative finish.

10. Place the rolls on a baking tray and brush with milk and then sprinkle with the remaining sugar and spice mix.

11. Bake for about 10-15 minutes until golden brown and puffy.

Carefully lift from the baking tray with an egg slice or palette knife. Best served warm.

PRIMROSE POTS

Cost: ££

Age: 7+

Small orange-flavoured sponge cakes with marzipan petals. Use the left-over sponge to make Hot Dreamy Trifle on page 127 or Chocolate Truffles on page 145.

Takes 1 hour to prepare
20 mins. to cook

Makes 5

You will need:
oil for greasing
100g soft margarine
100g white sugar
2 eggs, size 4
zest of 1 orange
50g wholemeal flour
50g plain white flour
1 teaspoon baking powder

Equipment:
pastry brush
18cm square cake tin
scales
2 table knives
mixing bowl
tablespoon
grater
wooden spoon
teaspoon

For the decoration:
50g soft margarine
75g icing sugar
vermicelli
75g marzipan
small sweet jellies or
  "Smarties"

sieve
oven gloves
wooden cocktail stick
cooling rack
small mixing bowl
6cm plain biscuit
  cutter
small dish
serving plate
pastry board
rolling pin
3cm plain cutter

Method

1. Preheat the oven to 350°F (180°C, gas mark 4). Grease the cake tin.

2. Put 100g of the margarine and sugar into a large mixing bowl with the eggs. Grate the zest of the orange, add that and beat well together with a wooden spoon.

3. Sieve the flours and baking powder into the mixture and fold them in.

4. Turn the mixture into the greased tin and spread level.

5. Bake in the centre of the oven for 15-20 minutes until golden and well risen. Test with a wooden cocktail stick inserted into the centre – it should come out clean when the cake is cooked.

6. Leave the cake in the tin for a few minutes and then turn out onto a wire cooling rack to cool.

7. Make the buttercream – beat the remaining margarine and the icing sugar together with the wooden spoon in a small bowl until smooth and soft. Leave on one side.

8. Cut rounds from the cold sponge cake using the large cutter. Put the off-cuts to one side and save for later use in another recipe.

9. Pour some vermicelli into a small flat dish. Take one of the rounds and spread a thin layer of the buttercream to cover

Fig. 51. Rolling in vermicelli

the sides and then roll this in the vermicelli to coat evenly.

10. Place the round on a plate and spread buttercream on the top to cover. Repeat these processes with all the rounds.

11. Knead the marzipan until softened and then roll it out thinly.

12. Use the small cutter and cut out 3 or 4 "petals" for each cake, and then shape them by pinching a small piece of the edge together between finger and thumb and then mark down the centre towards the pinched point with the back of a knife.

13. To finish the cakes, put one "Smartie" or jelly sweet in the centre of each cake and arrange 3 or 4 petals around these to represent primroses.

To store
These will keep well in an airtight tin for 5-7 days.

To freeze
Open freeze until solid, pack into a plastic box or bag. Seal, label and freeze for up to 3 months.

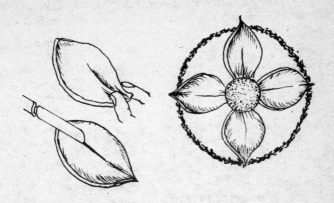

Fig. 52. Shaping the petals

To serve from frozen
Leave unwrapped at room temperature for about 2 hours.

To microwave   *Takes 1 hour to prepare*
                                         6 mins. to cook

1. Put 100g of the margarine and sugar into a large mixing
bowl with the eggs. Grate the zest of the orange, add that and
beat well together with a wooden spoon.

2. Sieve the flours and baking powder into the mixture and
fold them in.

3. Put about 1 tablespoonful of the mixture into microwave
muffin pans or individual small dishes or cups – do not fill
more than half full. Arrange cups or dishes in a circle on a
plate, 4 or 5 at a time and microwave on HIGH for
3 minutes.

4. Remove the cakes onto a wire cooling rack.

5. Follow Stages 7-13 of the Conventional Cooking
Method.

NEST CAKES

Cost: £

Age: 7+

These are very easy to make and decorate. Use tiny sweet Easter eggs for decoration, or have fun making your own from marzipan.

Takes 20 mins. to prepare   *Makes 9-10*
    or 45 mins. if making your own eggs

You will need:
25g margarine
1 tablespoon golden syrup
25g block cooking chocolate
1 tablespoon icing sugar
1 tablespoon coconut
approx. 75g crispies
18-20 miniature eggs OR
    50g marzipan

Equipment:
**bun tin or baking
    tray**
**9 or 10 paper cake
    cases**
small saucepan
table knife
2 tablespoons
scales
wooden spoon
pastry board

Method
1.   Set the paper cake cases out on a baking tray or bun tin.

2.   Put the margarine, syrup and chocolate into a saucepan over a gentle heat to melt it, stirring occasionally with a wooden spoon.

3.   Remove from the heat and add the icing sugar and coconut, stirring to mix.

4.   Finally, add not quite all of the crispies and stir to coat well in the chocolate. Add more if the sauce still looks fairly runny.

5.   Place spoonsfuls of the mixture in the cake cases,

Fig. 53. Hollowing the centres

hollowing the centre slightly to form nests.

6.   Place two eggs in each one and leave in a cool place to set.

Fig. 54. Puttings the eggs in

7.   If using marzipan for the eggs – work the marzipan with your hands until soft and then pinch a small piece off about the size of a sugar lump and shape into an egg. Repeat with the rest of the marzipan, making about 18 eggs. Place 2 eggs in each nest.

If time allows, the marzipan eggs may be painted with different food colours for more effect.

To store
In an airtight tin for 2-3 days.

To microwave   *Takes 15 mins. to prepare*
                              or 35 mins. if making your own eggs

1.   Put the margarine, syrup and chocolate into a basin and microwave on HIGH for 25-30 *seconds*. Leave to stand, stirring occasionally until smooth.

2.   Meanwhile, set the paper cake cases out on a baking tray or bun tin.

3.   Continue from Stage 3 of the Conventional Cooking Method to complete.

MINI SIMNEL CAKE

Cost: ££
                                                        Age: 7+

You will need a 454g tin of pineapple or ham! Open the tin carefully leaving no jagged edges – save the contents for tea and then use the washed-out tin to bake the cake in! The size of tin required is 10cm in diameter.

Takes 40 mins. to prepare   *Serves 6-8*
plus cooling time
*   45 mins. to cook*

You will need:	Equipment:
oil for greasing	**10cm diameter, deep**
50g soft margarine	** tin**
50g soft brown sugar	**pastry brush**
1 dessertspoon golden syrup	**scales**
1 egg, size 4	**mixing bowl**
75g plain white flour	**table knife**
½ teaspoon mixed spice	**tablespoon**
100g mixed dried fruit	**wooden spoon**
1 dessertspoon orange juice	**small bowl**
** OR milk**	**fork**

125-150g marzipan
approx. 1 dessertspoon
   apricot jam

sieve
teaspoon
2 dessertspoons
oven gloves
wooden cocktail stick
cooling rack
serving plate
pastry board
rolling pin

Method

1. Preheat the oven to 350°F (180°C, gas mark 4). Grease the tin.

2. Place the margarine, sugar and syrup in a large mixing bowl and beat together with a wooden spoon until smooth and light.

3. Break the egg into a small bowl and beat with a fork.

4. Add a little of the egg to the margarine mixture and beat in and then sieve a little of the flour in. Continue adding these alternately until all is used up.

5. Add the mixed spice and the fruit and mix well together.

6. Finally, add the orange juice or milk to make a fairly soft consistency. Place the mixture in the tin and make it level.

7. Bake in the centre of the oven for 40-45 minutes, testing with a wooden cocktail stick inserted into the centre – it will come out clean when the cake is cooked. Turn the cake onto a wire rack to cool completely. Put on a serving plate when cold.

8. Knead the marzipan gently on a pastry board until smooth and pliable and then use 25-50g of it and make into 11 small balls, each about the size of a marble. Leave on one side, and then roll out the remaining marzipan so that it fits the top of the cake.

9. Spread or brush a little apricot jam over the top of the cold cake and then place the rolled out marzipan over, making neat finished edges with your fingers and thumb (like

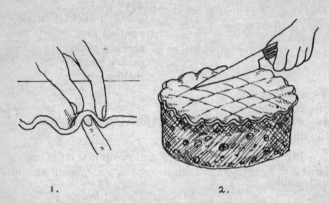

Fig. 55. (1) Making neat edges
(2) Making criss cross marks

a pie crust) and criss cross marks with a knife across the middle. Then place marzipan balls on the top, around the edge.

10. Preheat a grill, and then place the cake under it for 1-2 minutes just to brown the top of the marzipan a little.

Note: This cake has Biblical connections: the 11 marzipan balls represent the 11 Apostles, excluding Judas the betrayer.

To store
This cake will keep very well in an airtight tin for several weeks.

To freeze
After Stage 7, wrap in foil and a plastic bag, seal, label and freeze for up to 6 months.

To serve from frozen
Unwrap and leave at room temperature for 4 hours and then proceed to decorate from Stage 8 above.

EASTER BONNET BISCUITS

Cost: ££   *Age: 9+*

This is my variation of an idea I saw a few years ago. It is
quite fiddly, but fun to do.

Takes 1½ hours to prepare   *Makes about 20*
       20 mins. to cook

You will need:
50g soft margarine
50g white sugar
½ egg, beaten (size 4)
1 teaspoon grated lemon zest
100g plain white flour
little milk

For the decoration:
125g soft margarine
225g icing sugar
3 food colours
1 packet marshmallows
sugar flowers, jelly sweets,
   "Smarties", vermicelli,
   hundreds and thousands

Equipment:
scales
mixing bowl
table knife
tablespoon
wooden spoon
fork
3 small bowls
grater
teaspoon
sieve
pastry board
flour dredger
rolling pin
7cm plain biscuit
   cutter
baking trays
oven gloves
palette knife
cooling rack
cocktail stick

Method

1.   Preheat the oven to 350°F (180°C, gas mark 4).

2.   Put the margarine and sugar into a mixing bowl and beat
together with a wooden spoon until light and creamy.

3.   Break the egg into a small bowl and beat it well with a
fork and then add about 1½-2 tablespoonfuls to the
margarine mixture and beat it in.

4. Carefully grate the lemon to obtain 1 teaspoonful of zest and add this to the mixture and beat in.

5. Sieve and stir in the flour and mix to a stiff consistency. A very little milk may be needed to achieve this. The dough should not be sticky.

6. Sprinkle flour from a flour dredger onto a pastry board. Turn the dough onto the board and knead it gently until smooth and then roll out thinly (about 3mm) and cut out biscuit rounds with the cutter.

7. Place the rounds on baking trays, leaving space between each one to allow it to spread slightly, and cook for 15-20 minutes until it is turning a light golden colour.

8. Leave on the tray for 2-3 minutes and then transfer to a wire cooling rack with a palette knife.

Fig. 56.
Covering with buttercream
and the finished result

9. To make the buttercream – put the remaining margarine and the icing sugar into a bowl and beat together until smooth.

10. Divide this between 3 bowls and colour each one with a different colour, e.g. pink, blue, yellow or mauve.

11. To make a bonnet, use one colour of buttercream and put a little on the base of a marshmallow with a knife and then place it on a biscuit to stick together.

12. Cover the biscuit and marshmallow completely with a thin layer of the buttercream by spreading it over with a knife. Repeat with the rest of the biscuits and marshmallows, making a few of each colour.

13. Make lines all around the hats with a cocktail stick to give a straw effect.

14. Finish off by placing 2 or 3 sugar flowers or sweets at the crown. Vary them by also putting some vermicelli or hundreds and thousands around the brims of some of the hats.

To store
In an airtight tin for 2-3 days.

CHOCOLATE TRUFFLES

Cost: ££   *Age: 7+*

Serve as a special tea-time cake or as sweets made into a gift. They are rather rich.

Takes 45 mins. to prepare   *Makes about 20*

You will need:	*Equipment:*
150g plain cooking chocolate	**scales**
250g sponge (cake trimmings or stale cake)	**basin**
	small saucepan
3 tablespoons milk	**table knife**
about 1½ teaspoons brandy OR rum essence	**large bowl**
	tablespoon
50g raisins OR cherries	**teaspoon**

chocolate vermicelli   **chopping board**
  OR cocoa   **vegetable knife**
                          cereal dish
                          paper sweet cases

Method

1.   Break up the chocolate into small pieces and put into a basin fitted over a pan of hot water on a low heat to melt, stirring occasionally (see page 21).

2.   Meanwhile, crumble the cake by gently breaking it up with your fingers into a large bowl.

3. Add the milk, essence and melted chocolate to the crumbs and mix well together.

4.   Chop the raisins or cherries and add to the mixture. Combine well.

5.   Leave in the refrigerator until cool and slightly firmed (about 15-30 minutes).

6.   Put the vermicelli or cocoa into a small dish.

7.   Take a tablespoon of the mixture and roll into a ball-shape and then roll it in the vermicelli or cocoa to coat it. Place into sweet cases.

To freeze
Pack into a plastic box, cover, label and freeze for up to 3 months.

To serve from frozen
Place on a plate and leave at room temperature for about 1 hour.

To microwave   *Takes 40 mins. to prepare*

1.   Break up the chocolate into small pieces and put into a microwave-proof basin and microwave on HIGH for 2 minutes until melted, stirring after each minute.

2.   Follow Stages 2-7 of the Conventional Cooking Method to complete.

To make a gift
Follow the instructions at the end of recipes on pages 70, 106 or 107.

DAIRY DRINKS

Cost: £   *Age: 7+*

These quickly-made drinks have many possibilities in flavouring. Use whole, skimmed or semi-skimmed milk – or yoghurt. Try one of these variations – experiment!

CHOCOLATE MILK SHAKE

Takes 15 mins. to prepare   *Serves 4*

You will need: *Equipment:*
**3 tablespoons drinking   large bowl
  chocolate   tablespoon
3 tablespoons boiling   whisk or fork
  water   measuring jug
950ml chilled milk   4 tumblers
4-5 tablespoons vanilla
  ice-cream**

Method
1. Mix the drinking chocolate with the water in a large bowl until smooth.

2. Whisk in the milk and half the ice-cream.

3. Share the remaining ice-cream between 4 tumblers and fill with the milk mixture. Serve immediately.

FRUITY MILK SHAKE

Takes 15 mins. to prepare   *Serves 4*

You will need: *Equipment:*
**125ml fruit purée (rasp-   large bowl
    berry, strawberry,   tablespoon
    apricot)   whisk or fork
500ml chilled milk   measuring jug
icing sugar to taste   sieve
4 tablespoons ice-cream   4 tumblers**

Method

1.   Pour the purée into the bowl and whisk in the milk until thoroughly blended.

2.   Sweeten to taste by sieving in icing sugar and chill well in the refrigerator.

3.   Pour into 4 tumblers and top with 1 tablespoon of ice-cream in each one.

Try combining different flavours of fruit purée and ice-cream – e.g. raspberry and peach, strawberry and chocolate, apricot and orange or lemon.

FRUITY YOGHURT CUPS

Takes 10 mins. to prepare   *Serves 2*

You will need: *Equipment:*
**130g pineapple yoghurt   large bowl
250ml pineapple juice   whisk or fork
                                     measuring jug**

Method
1.   Pour the yoghurt into a large bowl and whisk in the fruit juice until well blended.

2.   Chill before serving. Pour into 2 tumblers.

OR

ORANGE YOGHURT CUP

130g orange yoghurt blended with **250ml orange juice**

OR

TROPICAL YOGHURT CUP

130g mixed yoghurt blended with **250ml tropical fruit juice**

OR

FRUITY YOGHURT COOLER

130g fruit yoghurt (any flavour) blended with **250ml chilled milk**

SUMMER

The Season for
Barbecues, Picnics,
Parties and Lunchboxes

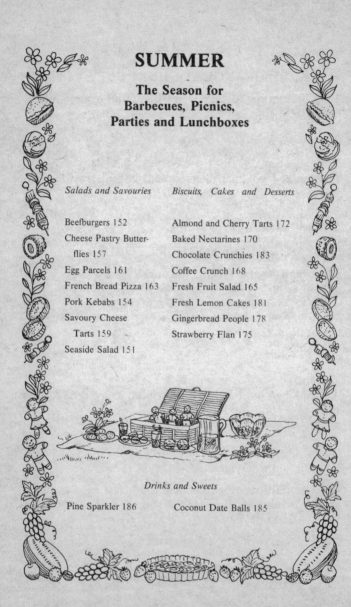

SEASIDE SALAD

Cost: ££   *Age: 7+*

This is a salad without lettuce – which you may think impossible!

Takes 25 mins. to prepare   *Serves 4*
       15 mins. to cook

You will need: *Equipment:*

75g pasta shells   **Large saucepan with**
2-3 tablespoons tinned peas   **lid**
2-3 tablespoons tinned sweet-   **scales**
** corn**   **colander**
200g tin tuna fish in oil   **serving dish**
75g thick set natural yoghurt   **tin opener**
1 tablespoon lemon juice   **tablespoon**
black pepper   **3 small bowls**
                                    fork

Method
1.   Fill the saucepan just over half full with cold water and bring to the boil. Add the pasta, cover with the lid and cook, simmering for 12-15 minutes until just tender.

2.   Drain and rinse in cold water, in a colander.

3.   Put into a serving dish and add the vegetables.

4.   Carefully open the tin of tuna, drain, reserving the oil in a small bowl and then flake the fish with a fork in another small bowl. Add to the pasta.

5.   Put the yoghurt into a separate small bowl with the lemon juice and about 1 tablespoon of the tuna oil and mix together to a thick runny consistency. Season to taste with the pepper.

6. Add this sauce to the pasta and vegetables and stir gently to coat.

Serve immediately with fresh crispy bread.

BEEFBURGERS

Cost: £   *Age:* 7+

Add your own favourite flavouring to top these, whether it's cheese, peanuts, pepper, relish or just ketchup!

Takes 30 mins. to prepare   *Serves 4*
       10 mins. to cook

You will need: *Equipment:*

450g lean minced beef   **mixing bowl**
salt and pepper   **teaspoon**
2 teaspoons mixed herbs   **tablespoon**
1 tablespoon Worcester sauce   **vegetable knife**
1 small onion   **chopping board**
1 egg, size 4   **grater**
                                       small bowl
                                       fork
                                       table knife

Method
1. Put the meat into a large mixing bowl and add a pinch or two of salt and pepper, the herbs and Worcester sauce.

2. Peel and wash the onion and either finely chop or grate it and then add to the meat. Mix together with a tablespoon.

3. Break the egg into a small bowl and beat with a fork and then add to the meat to bind it together.

4. Divide the mixture into 8 equal portions by marking it out with a knife while it's still in the bowl.

5. Wet your hands with cold water and take one portion with a tablespoon and shape it in your wet hands into a round flat cake. Place on the grill pan and repeat with the rest of the mixture.

6.   Preheat the grill to medium, and then cook the burgers for about 5 minutes until browned and then turn them over to cook a further 5 minutes to brown the other side.

Serve hot inside bread rolls or on a plate with potatoes and vegetables.

To freeze
Open freeze after Stage 5, before cooking, and then pack into plastic bags, seal, label and freeze for up to 2 months.

To serve from frozen
Preheat the grill to medium, and place the unwrapped burgers on the grill pan. Cook for about 5 minutes on each side until browned all over. (No need to thaw first.)

To microwave   *Takes 30 mins. to prepare*
                                   12 mins. to cook
1.   Make as in the Conventional Cooking Method, Stages 1-5.

2.   Place a piece of absorbent kitchen paper on a plate and then put 4 burgers in a circle on the top. Microwave on HIGH for 1½-3 minutes. Turn them over and cook for a further 1½-3 minutes. Repeat with the remaining 4 burgers.

Serve hot inside bread rolls or on a plate with potatoes and vegetables.

PORK KEBABS

Cost: ££   *Age:* 7+

These can be grilled or barbecued.

Marinade for 2-4 hours   *Serves 4*
Takes 30 mins. to prepare
*   10 mins. to cook*

You will need: *Equipment:*

2 tablespoons honey   **saucepan**
2 tablespoons soy sauce   **2 tablespoons**
1 tablespoon lemon juice   **chopping board**
500g lean pork (cut from   **vegetable knife**
**   the leg)**   **dish**
4 onions   **tin opener**
12-16 button mushrooms   **4 long metal**
12-16 pineapple cubes   **   skewers**
**   (tinned)**   **pastry brush**
                                     oven gloves
                                     serving dish

Method

1.   Make the marinade – put the honey, soy sauce and
lemon juice into a saucepan on a low heat and stir until the
honey is melted.

2.   Cut the meat into 2cm cubes using the vegetable knife
and chopping board, trimming off any pieces of fat.

3.   Put the meat into a shallow dish and pour the marinade
over, cover and leave for about 2-4 hours in the refrigerator,
turning the meat in the sauce several times.

4.   When you are ready to cook the kebabs, peel and wash
the onions. Cut them into quarters. Wipe the mushrooms
with a clean, damp cloth. Open the tin of pineapple carefully
(mind the sharp edges!) and strain off the juice which is not
needed.

(If microwaving, go to Stage 6, missing out Stage 5.

5.   Preheat the grill to medium.

6.   Assemble the kebabs on the skewers – thread the meat, onion, mushrooms and pineapple in turn and repeat until all

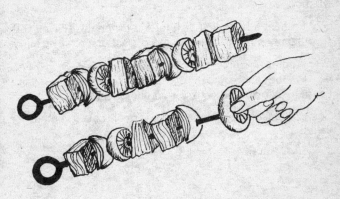

Fig. 57. Assembling the kebabs

is used up, sharing each ingredient equally between the 4 skewers.

(If microwaving, go to Stage 3 of the Microwave Method.)

7.   Brush with some of the remaining marinade and cook under the grill, turning and brushing with any remaining marinade several times, for about 10 minutes until browned all over and the meat is tender. *Remember to use oven gloves when turning the skewers.*

Serve immediately with cooked rice, baked potato or salad.

To microwave   *Marinade for 2-4 hours*
                                  Takes 30 mins. to prepare
                                       3 mins. to cook

Use long *wooden* skewers instead of metal skewers.

1.   Make the marinade – put the honey, soy sauce and lemon juice into a small bowl and microwave for a few seconds on HIGH to melt the honey. Stir and repeat if necessary.

2.   Follow Stages 2, 3, 4 and 6 of the Conventional Cooking Method.

3.   Preheat a browning dish for 5½-6 minutes (check with the manufacturer's instructions in your microwave handbook).

4.   Put the kebabs into the dish and cook for 2 minutes. Turn the kebabs over and cook for another 1 minute.

Serve immediately with cooked rice, baked potato or salad.

CHEESE PASTRY BUTTERFLIES

Cost: £   *Age: 7+*

These are attractive, easy-to-make finger foods which are suitable for parties and suppers.

Takes 45 mins. to prepare   *Makes lots!*
        10 mins. to cook

You will need: *Equipment:*

100g plain white flour   scales
1 teaspoon dry mustard   mixing bowl
pinch of salt   sieve
50g hard margarine   tablespoon
50g Cheddar or Leicester   teaspoon
  cheese   table knife
1 egg yolk   grater
1 tablespoon water   pastry board
about 75g cream cheese   flour dredger
fresh parsley   rolling pin
                                    4cm plain cutter
                                    2 baking trays
                                    oven gloves
                                    small bowl
                                    wooden spoon

Method
1.   Preheat the oven to 425°F (220°C, gas mark 7).

2.   Sieve the flour, mustard and salt into a large mixing bowl, add the margarine (cut into small pieces) and rub in until it resembles fine breadcrumbs.

3.   Carefully grate the cheese into the flour and margarine *(mind your fingers!)* and stir together.

4.   Bind together to form a firm dough with the egg yolk and water.

5. Sprinkle flour from a flour dredger onto a pastry board. Roll out the dough on the board to about ½cm thickness and cut into rounds with the pastry cutter, gathering up and repeating with the off-cuts, until all is used up.

6. Cut half of these into halves to become the "wings". Place the pastry rounds on a baking tray and cook for 7-10 minutes until slightly golden. Put the half rounds onto another baking tray and cook for 3-5 minutes until slightly golden. Leave on the baking trays until cold.

7. Put the cream cheese into a small bowl and beat with a wooden spoon until soft and smooth.

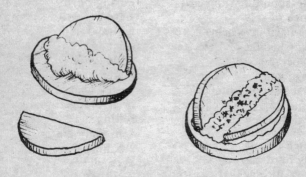

Fig. 58. Making the butterflies

8. To make the butterflies – put a teaspoonful of the cream cheese in the centre of the round biscuits and press the halved biscuits into position to make the wings. Sprinkle a little parsley on the cheese between the wings.

To store
In an airtight tin for 1-2 days.

To freeze
Before decorating, pack the biscuits into a plastic box or bag. Seal, label and freeze for up to 4 months.

To serve from frozen
Unwrap and place on a baking tray and crisp in a hot oven
(400°F, 200°C, gas mark 6) for 5-10 minutes, cool and then
decorate as Stage 8 above.

SAVOURY CHEESE TARTS

Cost: £   *Age: 7+*

Cheese pastry cases filled with different flavour fillings. Nice
for parties, picnics and lunchboxes.

Takes 45 mins. to prepare   *Makes about 12*
*   10 mins. to cook*

You will need:

100g plain white flour
1 teaspoon dry mustard
pinch of salt
50g hard margarine
50g Cheddar or Leicester
  cheese
1 egg yolk
1 tablespoon water

Fillings:
1-2 pilchards and
  1 teaspoon lemon juice
OR
about 75g corned beef and
  1 tablespoon mayonnaise
OR
about 50g lean ham and
  75g cream cheese

Equipment:

scales
mixing bowl
sieve
tablespoon
teaspoon
table knife
grater
pastry board
flour dredger
rolling pin
7cm plain pastry
  cutter
bun tins
3 forks
oven gloves
3 dishes
tin opener

Method

1. Preheat the oven to 425°F (220°C, gas mark 7).

2. Sieve the flour and mustard and salt into a large mixing bowl, add the margarine (cut into small pieces) and rub in until it resembles fine breadcrumbs.

3. Carefully grate the cheese into the flour and margarine *(mind your fingers!)* and stir together.

4. Bind together to form a firm dough with the egg yolk and water.

5. Sprinkle flour from a flour dredger onto a pastry board. Roll the dough out on the board to about 3mm thickness and cut into rounds with the pastry cutter. Gather up and repeat with the off-cuts until it's all used up.

6. Put the pastry rounds into the bun tins and prick the bases all over with a fork.

7. Bake blind for 5-10 minutes until turning golden. Leave in the bun trays until cold.

8. Make your chosen filling:

(1) Put the pilchards into a dish and mash with the lemon juice (remove the bones first if preferred); OR

(2) Mash the corned beef in a dish with the mayonnaise; OR

(3) Chop the ham into very small pieces and mix with the cream cheese.

9. Pile the filling into each pastry case, serve immediately.

To store
The pastry keeps well in an airtight tin if unfilled.

To freeze
Pack the pastry cases into a plastic box or bag. Seal, label and freeze for up to 4 months.

To serve from frozen
Put the pastry cases into the bun trays and crisp in a hot oven
(400°F, 200°C, gas mark 6) for 5-10 minutes. Cool and then
fill as in Stage 8.

EGG PARCELS

Cost: £   *Age: 7+*

A variation of sausage and egg which is oven-baked for
healthier eating rather than fried.

Takes 30 mins. to prepare   *Serves 2-4*
*   25 mins. to cook*

You will need: *Equipment:*
2 eggs, size 3   **small saucepan**
little flour and milk to coat   **3 dishes**
100g sausagemeat   **mixing bowl**
¼ teaspoon basil   **scales**
½ teaspoon sage   **teaspoon**
1-2 tablespoons crisp bread-   **fork**
**   crumbs**   **pastry board**
                                   baking tray
                                   oven gloves

Method
1.   Preheat the oven to 400°F (200°C, gas mark 6).

2.   Hard boil the eggs – put them in a saucepan and cover
with cold water. Put on a high heat, bring to the boil and then
reduce the heat to simmer for 10 minutes.

3.   Cool under running water, shell, wash and pat dry.

4.   Put the flour into a dish and roll each egg in it to
coat it.

5.   Put the sausagemeat into a mixing bowl, add the herbs
and mix together with a fork and then divide into 2 equal
portions.

6. Sprinkle a little flour onto a pastry board. Flatten each portion of the meat into an oblong shape on the board and then wrap each egg in the meat, sealing the ends and patting into a smooth shape.

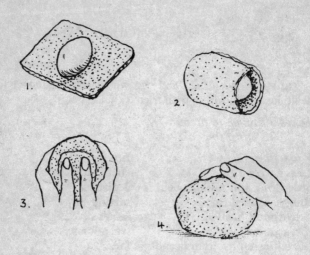

Fig. 59. Wrapping the eggs in meat

7. Pour the milk into a dish and put the breadcrumbs into a separate dish.

8. Roll each parcel first in the milk and then in the breadcrumbs to coat it.

9. Place on a baking tray and cook for 25 minutes.

Serve hot with potatoes and green vegetables or serve cold with a salad.

To store
In the refrigerator for 2-3 days.

FRENCH BREAD PIZZA

Cost: £   *Age: 7+*

This is a quick pizza to make from ingredients you may have
to hand in your stock cupboards.

Takes 30 mins. to prepare   *Serves 4*
       10 mins. to cook

You will need: *Equipment:*
1 onion   **chopping board**
1 green pepper   **vegetable knife**
100g lean ham OR **salami**   **scales**
1 tomato   **grater**
100g cheese   **tablespoon**
½ French stick   **teaspoon**
1 tablespoon tomato purée   **baking tray**
   OR ketchup   **oven gloves**
2 teaspoons mixed herbs   **plate**

Method
1.   Preheat the oven to 350°F (180°C, gas mark 4).

2.   Peel, wash and finely chop the onion with a vegetable
knife on a chopping board.

3.   Wash, remove the seeds and chop the pepper.

4.   Chop the meat. Slice the tomato.

5.   Carefully grate the cheese *(mind your fingers –
remember graters are sharp!)*.

6.   Cut the French stick in half horizontally and cut each
piece in half vertically (which means you now have 4
pieces).

7.   Spread the tomato purée over the bread.
(If microwaving, go to Stage 5 of the Microwave Method.)

8.   Put the chopped onion, pepper and meat onto the
bread.

9. Arrange the tomato slices on top of these and then sprinkle the cheese on the top.

Fig. 60. Arranging the pizza

10. Finally, sprinkle the herbs over it.

11. Bake for 10 minutes and serve immediately.

This may also be cooked on a barbecue.

To freeze
Wrap in foil and a plastic bag, seal, label and freeze for up to 2 months.

To serve from frozen
Remove the wrappings and place on a baking tray in a preheated oven at 400°F (200°C, gas mark 6) for about 20 minutes.

To microwave   *Takes 30 mins. to prepare*
(extra 15g margarine needed.)   *Takes 8 mins. to cook*

1. Peel, wash and finely chop the onion with a vegetable knife on a chopping board.

2. Wash, remove the seeds and chop the pepper.

3. Put the onion and pepper into a microwave-proof dish with 15 g margarine and cook on HIGH for 4 minutes, stirring once.

4. Follow Stages 4-7 of the Conventional Cooking Method.

5. Spread the onion and pepper mixture over the tomato base.

6. Put the meat pieces and then the tomato slices over the top and then sprinkle with the cheese.

7. Finally, sprinkle the herbs over it.

8. Place on a plate and microwave on HIGH for 4 minutes until the cheese has melted.

Serve immediately.

FRESH FRUIT SALAD

Cost: ££   *Age: 7+*

There are some delicious fruits available at reasonable prices which make gorgeous salads – there's a touch of the exotic in this one!

Takes 45 mins. to prepare   *Serves 4*

You will need:

1 nectarine
1 tablespoon lemon juice
1-2 slices pineapple
¼ melon (honeydew, water-
**   melon, galia)**
50g grapes
225g strawberries
1 kiwi

Equipment:

chopping board
vegetable knife
serving dish
colander
tablespoon

Method

1. Gently wipe over the nectarine with a clean, damp cloth, cut it in half, remove the stone and slice the fruit vertically.

Place in a serving dish and sprinkle with lemon juice to prevent it browning.

2. Cut the pineapple into bite-size pieces and add to the dish.

3. Remove the skin and seeds from the melon and cut the

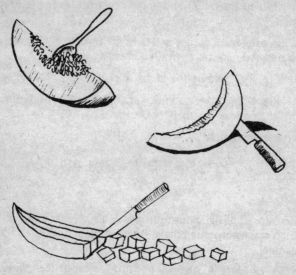

Fig. 61. Preparing the melon

fruit into bite-size pieces and add to the dish.

4. Wash the grapes, cut in half and remove any pips and then place in the dish.

5. Pull out the hulls (stalks and green bits) from the strawberries and drain them well in a colander and then cut into halves or quarters, depending upon their size. Place them in the dish.

6. Peel the kiwi thinly, removing as little of the flesh as

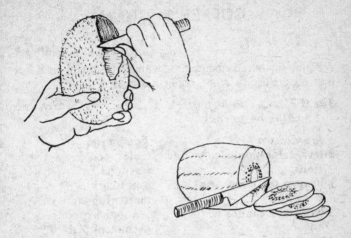

Fig. 62. Peeling and slicing the kiwi fruit

possible. Slice the fruit horizontally and add to the dish.

7. Very gently mix all the fruit together.

Serve with Greek yoghurt, pouring cream or ice-cream.

To store
Although this is best eaten fresh it may be kept covered in the refrigerator for 2-3 days.

To freeze
Pour into a plastic container, seal with a lid, label and freeze for up to 12 months.

To serve from frozen
Leave at room temperature for about 8 hours or in a refrigerator overnight. The fruit will be softer than when fresh, having lost its bite.

COFFEE CRUNCH

Cost: £   *Age:* 7+

A coffee-flavoured custard base with a crunchy topping. For best results use "Camp" coffee essence.

Takes 25 mins. to prepare   *Serves 6*
*   20 mins. to cook*

You will need: *Equipment:*
2 level tablespoons corn-   **tablespoon**
** flour**   **teaspoon**
1 heaped teaspoon drinking   **saucepan**
** chocolate**   **measuring jug**
3 level tablespoons white   **2 wooden spoons**
** sugar**   **ovenproof dish (0.75**
300ml milk   ** litre)**
3 tablespoons coffee essence   **mixing bowl**
** ("Camp")**   **scales**
                                         table knife
For the topping: **plastic bag and**
50g soft margarine   ** tie-tag**
1 level tablespoon white   **rolling pin**
** sugar**   **oven gloves**
50g digestive biscuits
50g wheat flakes

Method
1.   Preheat the oven to 325°F (170°C, gas mark 3).

2.   Put the cornflour, drinking chocolate and sugar into a saucepan.

3.   Add about 3 tablespoonfuls of the milk and blend together with a wooden spoon until smooth and all the lumps are worked out. Stir in the remaining milk and then the coffee essence.

4.   Cook over a fairly high heat, stirring all the time with the wooden spoon until it boils and thickens. Remove from the heat and pour into the pie dish.

5. Put the margarine into a mixing bowl with the sugar and beat together with a wooden spoon.

6. Put the biscuits into a plastic bag and secure with the tie-tag and then crush with a rolling pin (see page 66). Add the biscuits to the margarine and sugar and mix together.

7. Put the wheat flakes into the plastic bag, secure and crush with the rolling pin. Add to the margarine mixture and mix together.

8. Spoon the crumb mixture over the top of the custard and make level.

(If microwaving, go to Stage 6 of the Microwave Method.)

9. Bake in the centre of the oven for 10-15 minutes until the topping is beginning to brown.

Serve hot or cold with cream.

To microwave   *Takes 25 mins. to prepare*
                                        14 mins. to cook

1. Put the cornflour, drinking chocolate and sugar into a tall microwave-proof jug and blend with about 3 table-spoonfuls of the milk until smooth and all the lumps are worked out.

2. Stir in the remaining milk and then the coffee essence.

3. Microwave on HIGH for 5-6 minutes, stirring every 2 minutes, until the custard is thick and smooth.

4. Pour into a microwave-proof dish and leave on one side.

5. Follow Stages 5-8 of the Conventional Cooking Method.

6. Microwave on HIGH for 5 minutes and then flash under a hot grill to brown for 2-3 minutes if desired.

Serve hot or cold with cream.

BAKED NECTARINES

Cost: ££   *Age: 7+*

Tinned peaches may be used if nectarines are unavailable.

Takes 25 mins. to prepare   *Serves 4*
*   20 mins. to cook*

You will need: *Equipment:*
25g soft margarine   **mixing bowl**
2 tablespoons white sugar   **scales**
25g biscuits (digestive or   **tablespoon**
**   rich tea)**   **table knife**
25g ground almonds OR   **wooden spoon**
**   hazelnuts**   **plastic bag**
few drops almond essence   **tie-tag**
4 nectarines   **rolling pin**
                                 vegetable knife
                                 chopping board
                                 teaspoon
                                 ovenproof dish
                                 tin opener
                                 oven gloves

Method

1. Preheat the oven to 325°F (170°C, gas mark 3).

2. Put the margarine and sugar into a mixing bowl and cream together with a wooden spoon.

3. Put the biscuits into a plastic bag, secure with a tie-tag and then crush with a rolling pin (see page 66). Add the biscuits to the creamed mixture.

4. Add the nuts and essence and mix well together. Leave on one side.

5. Cut the nectarines in half using a vegetable knife and chopping board, take out the stones and make the centres slightly larger by scooping out some of the flesh with a teaspoon. Add this to the nut mixture and mix well. If using tinned peaches, drain off the juice and then scoop out the centres in the same way as above, adding the flesh to the nut mixture.

(If microwaving, go to Stage 2 of the Microwave Method.)

6.   Fill the nectarine halves with the nut mixture and place

Fig. 63. Filling the nectarine halves
with the nut mixture

in the ovenproof dish.

7.   Bake for 15-20 minutes or until the fruit feels tender when tested with a knife point.

Serve warm with Greek yoghurt.

To microwave   *Takes 25 mins. to prepare*
                                        5 mins. to cook

1.   Follow Stages 2-5 of the Conventional Cooking Method.

2.   Fill the nectarine halves with the nut mixture and place in a microwave-proof dish, cover with clingfilm and make 3 or 4 holes in it.

3.   Microwave on HIGH for 5¼ minutes or until the fruit feels tender when tested with the point of a knife.

Serve warm with Greek yoghurt.

ALMOND AND CHERRY TARTS

Cost: ££   *Age:* 7+

A sweet pastry base, a little jam, covered with a delicous light almond and cherry topping.

Takes 45 mins. to prepare   *Makes 15*
*   15 mins. to cook*

You will need: *Equipment:*
75g soft margarine   scales
50g white sugar   mixing bowl
1 egg yolk   table knife
75g wholemeal flour   2 tablespoons
75g plain white flour   wooden spoon
water to bind   sieve
                                    pastry board
For the topping: flour dredger
2 tablespoons red jam   rolling pin
50g soft margarine   7½cm pastry cutter
50g white sugar   bun tins
1 egg   teaspoon
almond essence   small bowl
50g ground almonds   oven gloves
50g rice flour OR ground rice   cooling rack
25g glacé cherries
icing sugar (sieved)

Method
1.   Preheat the oven to 350°F (180°C, gas mark 4).

2.   Put 75g soft margarine and 50g white sugar into a mixing bowl, add the egg yolk and beat well with a wooden spoon until light and fluffy.

3.   Sieve and mix in the flours, adding about 1 tablespoonful of cold water if necessary to bind it all together to form a firm dough.

4. Sprinkle flour from a flour dredger onto a pastry board. Turn the dough onto the board and knead it gently until smooth.
(If microwaving, go to Stage 2 of the Microwave Method.)

5. Roll it out to about 3mm in thickness and, using the pastry cutter, cut rounds to line the bun tins, gathering up and re-rolling the off-cuts until all are used up.

6. Spread ½ teaspoonful of jam in the base of each pastry case.

7. Make the topping – put the remaining margarine, sugar, whole egg and a few drops of essence into a bowl and beat together with a wooden spoon until creamy.

8. Fold in the almonds and rice flour. Chop the cherries finely and add to the mixture. Mix together.
(If microwaving, go to Stage 7 of the Microwave Method.)

9. Spread a heaped teaspoonful of the mixture over the jam in each pastry case.

Fig. 64. Stage 9

10. Bake in the centre of the oven for 12-15 minutes until well risen and golden brown.

11. Cool on a wire cooling tray and then lightly cover with sieved icing sugar.

To store
In an airtight tin for up to 2 weeks.

To freeze
Cool, pack in plastic bags, seal, label and freeze for up to 4 months.

To serve from frozen
Unwrap and leave at room temperature for about 1 hour.

To microwave   *Takes 45 mins. to prepare*
                                       10 mins. to cook

Better results are obtained by making a large tart and cutting it into wedges.

1. Follow Stages 2-4 of the Conventional Cooking Method.

2. Roll out the dough to about 3mm in thickness and line a 21cm dish with it, trimming to neaten it.

3. Put a piece of absorbent kitchen paper in the pastry case and weight it down with a saucer.

4. Microwave on HIGH for 4 minutes, remove the saucer and paper and cook for a further 1 minute.

5. Spread the jam over the base of the pastry case.

6. Make the topping by following Stages 7 and 8 of the Conventional Cooking Method.

7. Spread the topping over the jam and microwave for 5 minutes on HIGH.

8. Leave to cool and then lightly cover with sieved icing sugar. Cut into wedges.

STRAWBERRY FLAN

Cost: £   *Age: 7+*

A crisp sweet pastry base combined with the fresh fruit flavour of summer.

Takes 45 mins. to prepare   *Serves 6*
*   15-25 mins. to cook*

You will need: *Equipment:*
65g soft margarine   **scales**
25g white sugar   **mixing bowl**
1 egg yolk   **table knife**
75g plain white flour   **2 tablespoons**
50g wholemeal flour   **wooden spoon**
cold water   **sieve**
250g fresh strawberries   **pastry board**
2 heaped tablespoons orange   **flour dredger**
** jelly marmalade**   **rolling pin**
                                    15-18cm flan tin OR
                                    ** a bun tray**
                                    fork
                                    oven gloves
                                    colander
                                    serving plate
                                    small saucepan
                                    pastry brush

Method
1.   Preheat the oven to 425°F (220°C, gas mark 7).

2.   Put the margarine and sugar into a mixing bowl and beat together with a wooden spoon until light and creamy.

3.   Beat in the egg yolk and then sieve and mix in the flours until the mixture comes together in a ball, leaving the bowl clean. A very small amount of cold water may be needed at this stage to achieve this.

4.   Sprinkle flour from a flour dredger onto a pastry board. Turn the dough onto the board and knead it gently until smooth.

(If microwaving, go to Stage 2 of the Microwave Method.)

5.   Roll out the pastry to fit the flan tin. Line the tin with the pastry and then prick the base all over with a fork. Bake blind for 15-20 minutes until turning golden.

6.   Alternatively, roll out the pastry and then cut with a 7cm pastry cutter to line a bun tray with individual pastry cases, prick the bases with a fork and bake for about 10 minutes.

7.   Allow the flan case, or individual cases, to cool completely in the tin and then carefully place on a serving plate.

8.   Pull out the hulls (stalks and green bits) from the strawberries. Wash and then drain them well in a colander. Cut into slices.

9.   When the pastry is cold arrange the strawberry slices, overlapping each other, to cover the base completely.

Fig. 65. How to arrange the strawberry slices

(If microwaving, go to Stage 5 of the Microwave Method.)

10. In a small saucepan, gently melt the marmalade over a low heat and then brush over the fruit to glaze.

Eat the same day.

To freeze
Strawberries are best not frozen – they go mushy. To freeze a pastry case, cool and then wrap it gently in foil and a plastic bag, seal, label and freeze for up to 4 months.

To serve from frozen
Unwrap, place on a serving dish and leave at room temperature for 1 hour, and then proceed to fill as from Stage 8 above.

To microwave   *Takes 45 mins. to prepare*
                                         9 mins. to cook

1. Follow Stages 2-4 of the Conventional Cooking Method.

2. Roll out the pastry to fit a flan dish. Line the dish with the pastry and then place two pieces of absorbent kitchen paper over the base, easing it into the corner between the base and side of the dish.

3. Microwave on HIGH for 5½-6 minutes, remove the paper and cook for further 1½-2½ minutes. The pastry should look puffy and the base appear dry when cooked. Leave to cool.

4. Follow Stages 8 and 9 of the Conventional Cooking Method.

5. Put the marmalade into a small bowl and microwave on HIGH for 30 *seconds,* stir and repeat if necessary and then brush over the fruit to glaze.

GINGERBREAD PEOPLE

Cost: £   *Age: 7+*

This is an old favourite to make – try decorating them with piped icing to give hair, faces, bows, hands, shoes, etc.

Takes 40 mins. to prepare   *Makes 4-6*
        10 mins. to cook

You will need: *Equipment:*
40g soft margarine   scales
40g soft brown sugar   mixing bowl
1½ tablespoons golden syrup   table knife
100g plain white flour   2 tablespoons
½ teaspoon baking powder   wooden spoon
½ teaspoon bicarbonate of   sieve
  soda   teaspoon
1¼ teaspoons ginger   pastry board
cherries, currants   flour dredger
ready-to-use-tube icing   rolling pin
                                    people biscuit cutter
                                       OR stiff paper,
                                       pencils, scissors
                                    baking trays
                                    egg slice
                                    oven gloves
                                    cooling rack

Method
1. Preheat the oven to 400°F (200°C, gas mark 6).

2. Put the margarine, sugar and syrup into a large mixing bowl and beat together with a wooden spoon until soft and creamy.

3. Sieve in the flour, baking powder, bicarbonate of soda and add the ginger and mix it all in. Then knead it thoroughly with your hand to combine the last bit together until it is smooth and leaves the bowl clean.

4. Sprinkle flour from a flour dredger onto a pastry board. Turn the dough onto the board and roll it out to about 5 mm in thickness. Cut out the shapes of boys and girls (if you have no cutters of these shapes, draw and cut out the shapes on stiff paper and then cut around these with a knife).

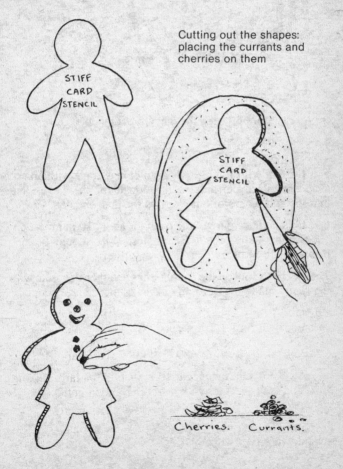

Cutting out the shapes: placing the currants and cherries on them

Fig. 66 Icing the gingerbread people

5. Carefully lift the biscuits onto baking trays with an egg slice and place currants in the dough for their eyes and buttons and pieces of cut cherries for their mouths.

6. Bake in the centre of the oven for about 10 minutes, but check them after about 6 minutes; they should be just beginning to brown.

7. Leave to cool on the baking trays and then decorate with the ready-made tube of icing to make them into "people".

To store
In an airtight tin for 2-3 weeks.

FRESH LEMON CAKES

Cost: £   *Age:* 7+

These cakes have a really fresh lemon taste and a crunchy topping.

Takes 30 mins. to prepare   *Makes 24*
     15 mins. to cook

You will need: *Equipment:*
oil for greasing   **Swiss roll tin**
150g soft margarine   **(30 x 20cm)**
150g white sugar   **pastry brush**
2 lemons   **scales**
2 eggs, size 4   **mixing bowl**
150g white self-raising   **table knife**
    flour   **2 tablespoons**
100g granulated sugar   **wooden spoon**
                              grater
                              2 small bowls
                              fork
                              sieve
                              oven gloves
                              lemon squeezer

Method
1.   Preheat the oven to 350°F (180°C, gas mark 4). Grease the tin.

2.   Put the margarine and 150g of the sugar into a mixing bowl and beat together with a wooden spoon until light and creamy. Grate the lemon zest into the mixture and mix in. *(Mind your fingers on the sharp grater!)*

3.   Break the eggs into a small bowl and beat them well with a fork. Gradually add them to the margarine mixture, a little at a time, beating well after each addition. Sieve and fold in the flour.

4. Turn the mixture into the tin and spread it out evenly.

(If microwaving, go to Stage 2 of the Microwave Method.)

5. Bake in the centre of the oven for about 15 minutes until golden and well risen.

6. Meanwhile, squeeze the juice from the lemons into a small bowl and mix with the remaining sugar.

7. Immediately the cake is taken out of the oven, spread the lemon and sugar mixture over it to cover it and leave it to cool in the tin.

8. When completely cold, cut into 24 slices – make 3 cuts down the length of the tin and 5 cuts across the width.

To store
In an airtight tin for 2-3 days.

To freeze
Open freeze on baking trays, then put into plastic bags or boxes. Seal, label and freeze for up to 6 months.

To serve from frozen
Remove the wrapping, place on a plate and leave at room temperature for about 1 hour.

To microwave   *Takes 30 mins. to prepare*
                                        7-8 mins. to cook
                                        plus standing time

1. Follow Stages 2-4 of the Conventional Cooking Method, but use a 21 cm square microwave-proof dish.

2. Microwave on HIGH for 7½ minutes, turning it 3 times if your oven is not fitted with a turntable. Let it stand for 5 minutes and then test with a wooden cocktail stick inserted into the sponge – it will come out clean when the cake is cooked. If it is not quite done, then microwave it for a few more seconds.

3. Meanwhile, squeeze the juice from the lemons into a small bowl and mix with the remaining sugar.

4. Immediately the cake is cooked sufficiently, spread the lemon and sugar mixture over it to cover it and leave it to cool in the dish.

5. When completely cold, cut into 25 slices, by making 4 cuts each way across the dish.

CHOCOLATE CRUNCHIES

Cost: £   *Age: 7+*

This recipe is a variation of one from my own school days! They are biscuits with a crisp crunchy coating and melt-in-the-mouth chocolate-flavoured centre.

Takes 30 mins. to prepare   Makes 12
       10 mins. to cook

You will need:	*Equipment:*
25g cornflakes	**scales**
100g soft margarine	**dish**
50g white sugar	**tablespoon**
vanilla essence	**2 table knives**
100g plain white flour	**mixing bowl**
1 tablespoon cocoa OR carob	**wooden spoon**
6 glacé cherries, halved	**sieve**
	baking tray
	oven gloves
	palette knife
	cooling rack

Method

1. Preheat the oven to 375°F (190°C, gas mark 5).

2. Put the cornflakes into a dish and crush them lightly with the back of a spoon.

3. Put the margarine and sugar into a mixing bowl and beat together with a wooden spoon and then mix in 2 or 3 drops of essence (dropped from the end of a teaspoon, not directly from the bottle, to control the amount).

4. Sieve in the flour and add the cocoa or carob and mix well.

5. Divide the mixture in half and then each half into 6 portions by marking out in the bowl with a knife.

6. Wet your hands with cold water and then take one portion of the mixture and roll it into a ball shape and then roll it in the cornflakes to coat it.

7. Place it on a baking tray and flatten slightly, then press half a cherry in the centre.

8. Repeat with the remaining portions of the biscuit mixture, leaving plenty of space between each one to allow them to spread out during cooking.

9. Bake in the centre of the oven for 8-10 minutes until beginning to brown slightly.

10. Leave to harden slightly on the baking tray and then place carefully on a wire cooling rack with a palette knife, to cool.

To store
These will keep in an airtight tin for about 1 week.

COCONUT DATE BALLS

Cost: ££   *Age:* 7+

Sweets are always a favourite to make – these are no exception! They are quick and easy and do not need cooking.

Takes 25 mins. to prepare   *Makes 15*

You will need:
50g cream cheese
100g icing sugar
50g coconut
50g dates
vanilla essence

Equipment:
scales
small bowl
wooden spoon
table knife
tablespoon
sieve
small dish
chopping board
vegetable knife
teaspoon

Method
1. Put the cream cheese into a bowl and beat with a wooden spoon until soft and creamy.

2. Sieve 1 tablespoon of icing sugar into a small dish and leave on one side.

3. Sieve the remaining icing sugar into the creamed cheese and blend in.

4. Add the coconut and mix in.

5. Finely chop the dates and add to the cheese mixture with a few drops of essence and mix well together.

6. Take 1 teaspoonful of the mixture and roll it in the reserved icing sugar to make a small ball.

Place in a paper sweet case. Repeat with the rest of the mixture.

To store
In a covered container or the refrigerator for a few days.

PINE SPARKLER

Cost: £   *Age: 7+*

This is a delicious thirst-quenching drink for warm summer
days.

Takes 10 mins. to prepare   *Serves 4*

You will need: *Equipment:*
2 tablespoons icing sugar   **large bowl**
5-6 tablespoons lemon juice   **tablespoon**
1 litre pineapple juice,   **whisk OR fork**
   chilled   **measuring jug**
500ml bitter lemon, chilled   **4 tumblers**
lemon slices (optional)

Method
1. Put the icing sugar into a large bowl and mix with the
lemon juice until smooth, using a whisk or fork.

2. Gradually stir in the pineapple juice and then the bitter
lemon.

3. Pour into tumblers and serve immediately with lemon
slices floating on top.

INDEX

Readers may be interested in the wide range of Paperfronts available. A full
catalogue can be had by sending S.A.E. to the address below.

ELLIOT RIGHT WAY BOOKS, KINGSWOOD, SURREY, U.K.